The Saint Louis
Art Museum
Handbook
of the Collections

The Saint Louis
Art Museum
Handbook
of the Collections

The Saint Louis Art Museum

1991

This publication was generously
supported by The Andrew W. Mellon
Foundation.

Mary Ann Steiner, editor
Maria Teresa Vicens, assistant editor
Katy Homans, designer
Patricia Woods, photography manager
Bob Kolbrener, Robert Pettus, Bill Selley,
David Ulmer, photographers

The Handbook was written by members
from the Museum's staff of curators and
educators: Janet C. Berlo, James D. Burke,
David Butler, Barbara Butts,
Sidney M. Goldstein, Elizabeth Horton,
Judith Weiss Levy, Judith W. Mann,
Kristan McKinsey, Laura Meyer,
Elizabeth W. Millard, Christina Nelson,
John W. Nunley, Steven D. Owyoung,
Joyce Schiller, Michael E. Shapiro,
Amanda Slavin, and Laurie A. Stein.

**Library of Congress Cataloguing
in Publication Data**
The Saint Louis Art Museum

The Saint Louis Art Museum
Handbook of the Collections
1. Art – Missouri –
The Saint Louis Art Museum.
2.The Saint Louis Art Museum –
Catalogue
LCC 90-064259   ISBN 0-89178-034-0

Cover:
Pablo Picasso, Spanish, 1881–1973
Pitcher and Fruit Bowl, 1931 (detail)
Oil on canvas
Bequest of Morton D. May 932:1983

Printed in Japan
by Toppan Printing Company

Contents

Foreword

Every museum justifiably proclaims its distinctive history. Ours has been defined by a special tradition of dedication to the art of the present, a global view of art and culture, a long and distinguished record of educational programming, and a noteworthy history of public ownership.

In its early years, the St. Louis Museum and School of Fine Arts (1879–1904) was strongly influenced by the Victoria and Albert Museum of London. The two museums shared a broad definition of art that included not only painting and sculpture but decorative arts; they were firmly committed to the art of the present. Both institutions operated in the hope that art would work with the burgeoning roles of science and industry for the betterment of every level of society. Halsey Cooley Ives, the Museum's founding director, defined his museum's policy in 1883, stating that it was "aimed directly to encourage branches of art which are living among us." He instructed us to pay heed "not only to paintings and sculptures, but also (to) the allied arts." Insisting on high standards of quality, he sought works of art and exhibitions that would illustrate "the highest standards of artistic intelligence and achievement of today."

This emphasis on art from one's own time was evident in the exhibits from the St. Louis World's Fair in 1904. At the Fair, the Art Palace exhibits were filled with art from the present day, not of the past, as most previous fairs had done. Virtually all the artists whose work was shown in the 1904 Fair were living. The Museum's enduring interest in the art of the present day was further demonstrated as collections grew after the World's Fair.

The period before 1920 was very successful in acquiring works by American artists, especially the followers of French Impressionism. Every major name in the American Impressionist movement is included, from Childe Hassam and William Merritt Chase to J. Alden Weir and Frederick Frieseke. By 1915, the Museum had acquired its first Monet, directly from the artist's dealer.

The Museum's record shows that works by Carl Milles, Thomas Hart Benton, Pablo Picasso, Marc Chagall, Henri Matisse, Alexander Calder, Max Beckmann, David Smith, Ansel Adams, Laura Gilpin, and Georgia O'Keeffe were all acquired by the Museum not only during the artists' lifetimes, but at vibrant moments within their careers. The Museum has continued to acquire works by notable living American artists, including Mark Rothko, Ellsworth Kelly, and Roy Lichtenstein; more recent acquisitions have included works by Susan Rothenberg, Gerhard Richter, and Anselm Kiefer. These judicious and well-timed acquisitions have helped build a strong collection of post-1960 paintings and sculpture. And with the help of collectors in our community, we have assembled an outstanding body of modern German painting; indeed, The Saint Louis Art Museum has the largest holdings of works by the German artist Max Beckmann in the world.

Such a tradition challenges the Museum's board and staff to differentiate among artists of the present day in its attempt to select art that will endure.

Despite the caprices of fashion, the Museum has sought to make judgments in the present that would provide outstanding works of art for the generations yet to come. Although funds have always been limited, there is a proven record of the highest artistic quality. This program also has been reflected in the Museum's schedule of special exhibitions. From 1906 to 1946, an effort was made to encourage American artists by presenting over forty annual group exhibits. In addition, many meritorious individuals were singled out for the special recognition of a one-person show. Some artists so honored included Joaquin Sorolla, Childe Hassam, Paul Manship, Hiro Yoshida, Carl Milles, and Max Beckmann. This tradition continues in the form of small, one-person exhibitions. And, it is encouraged with the long-term growth of an audience of those who greatly enjoy the Museum's energetic interest in art after Impressionism.

On a parallel track, the Museum's comprehensive holdings continued to grow from the beginning. This inclusive view of world civilization initially focused on Europe and Asia, as well as North America. Important Chinese works were acquired as early as 1919 and provide the foundation for one of the more important collections of Chinese bronzes in North America. The 1920s saw additions of nineteenth-century American paintings, ancient and Islamic art, important European paintings and sculptures, and the beginnings of a fine collection of drawings and prints. By the 1930s, the Decorative Arts and Medieval collections began to grow, and works from modernist movements were included acquisitions. This relatively varied outlook continues, for the Museum still embraces the values to be found in the great traditions of the past. Our educational programming continues to focus

on a universal history of art. In fact, the Museum's collection has become unusually well known for its holdings of the arts of Africa, Oceania, the native cultures of North America, and the cultures of Central and South America before the Spanish conquest, items more often consigned to ethnographic museums rather than art museums. Both the historical and diversified collections coexist harmoniously with the Museum's commitment to the present.

The Saint Louis Art Museum is the first publicly funded art museum in the United States. Today it is common to find municipal or regional public funding for art museums; some are much more extensively funded than we. St. Louis is unique, however, in that the rates are set in open elections; the use of funds is strictly controlled; and the entire museum is in public ownership. Accordingly, no general admission can be charged, a legacy from 1904.

The St. Louis Museum and School of Fine Arts was founded in 1879 as the first museum west of the Mississippi. A department of Washington University, it had seriously outgrown its old quarters by the turn of the century. As the Louisiana Purchase Exposition was planned, the Board determined that its lasting gift to the City would be a new art museum building. The Fair's president, David Francis, called it "the one material monument" deriving from the Exposition.

In 1907, under the provisions of the Missouri Legislature, the voters in the City of St. Louis established a publicly owned museum. The art school remained with the University, while the Museum was to be founded by a property tax that would be assessed in a public election. Its approval began a long public-private partnership that has endured through the century. Tax support was augmented by private investment, particularly in the building of the collections through bequests and gifts of works of art, and later through the creation of the membership organization, the Friends. In 1971 public support was expanded, to increase the base of support for the Museum and neighboring Zoo, also publicly owned. The result was the Metropolitan Zoological Park and Museum District, established by an act of the state government, funded by a public election in that year. This district included all of St. Louis County, as well as the City, and set the stage for the revival and growth of the Art Museum. In the mid-1960s, the programs had to be unusually limited, and the Museum facility was in serious need of renovation. By the mid-1970s, an extensive program of renovation and expansion was undertaken, mainly developed from private sources. A plan for support from the private sector was initiated, membership increased, and endowment funds were established. The voters approved an increase in public funding in 1983, as a broad endorsement of the expanded program, renovated facilities, and the enhanced stature of the Museum in the community. By the end of the 1980s, over $80 million dollars had been raised from private sources since the establishment of the Museum District, and income from taxes was exceeded by fund raising from other sources. Public funds were then accounting for less than forty-seven percent of total expense.

Over nearly fourteen years, the Museum completely renovated and restored its facilities. By 1989, installations were complete, and the comprehensive Museum once again available for public use. A comprehensive master plan was adopted then, embracing the concept of a balance between a historical past and dynamic present, and calling for renewed efforts in public education as well as in multicultural programming. Steady growth in Museum attendance has been an excellent indicator of public interest, particularly enhanced by the presentation of major travelling exhibitions in recent years.

As an institution, we still view ourselves as an educational tool for the community, as well as an important attraction in the area. People come to this Museum not only for the pleasures and challenges in the appreciation of art, but also for a greater understanding of art and culture. What this Museum, which ranks first in the nation in providing its population with educational services, can offer its visitors is a beautifully restored building installed with extraordinary works of art, an energetic schedule of special exhibitions, and a full program of performances, lectures, and educational services. We hope the Handbook is both an introduction and a welcome to The Saint Louis Art Museum.

James D. Burke
Director

Ancient
and
Islamic Arts

■

Bearded Bull's Head, c.2600–2550 B.C.
Near Eastern, Sumerian
Copper with lapis lazuli and seashell
Height: 9¼ in. (23.5 cm.)
Purchase: Friends Fund 260:1951

The chief Sumerian deity of the third
millennium B.C. was the sky-god An,
frequently depicted as a bull. As god of
fertility and power, he was believed to
be the source of vegetation and secular
authority. The bearded bull remained a
symbol of royal might throughout centuries of ancient Near Eastern art. Metal
sculpture from such an early period is
rare, since the costly materials were available only to elite craftsmen. This piece,
cast of copper, probably was attached
originally to a large lyre or harp of very
elaborate design.

■

Striding Man, c.2345–2195 B.C.
Egyptian, Old Kingdom, Sixth Dynasty
Wood
Height: 16 in. (40.6 cm.)
Purchase: Friends Fund 1:1986

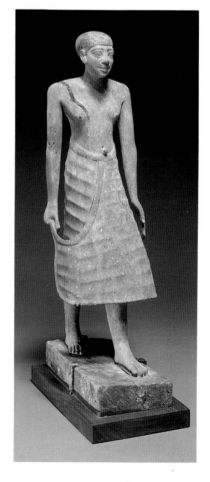

Most statues that survive Egypt's Old
Kingdom are made of stone, since wood-
en pieces were often severely damaged by
natural conditions such as rot and insects, not to mention the destruction
wrought by tomb robbers in search of
riches. This striding figure is a remarkable survivor.

The statue, one of a type known from
tombs at Saqqara, Memphis, and Giza,
probably represents a nobleman or an
official. He walks forward with assurance
and certainty, grasping the loose end
of his kilt and pulling it aside in an elegant flourish. This action may represent
a gesture of adoration or supplication
befitting a member of the nobility or
someone of high rank. The figure is notable for the subtle modeling of the body
beneath the pleated skirt and the exquisite
rendering of the hands. Also distinctive
are the inlaid nipples and skirt knot.

Cartonnage of Amen-Nestawy-Nakht,
c.930–880 B.C.
Egyptian, Thebes, Third Intermediate
Period, Early 22nd Dynasty
Linen, plaster, and pigments
Length: 66 in. (167.6 cm.)
Gift of Mr. and Mrs. Barney A. Ebsworth
for the children of St. Louis 109:1989

Amen-Nestawy-Nakht, a priest of Amun
at Thebes, was buried in a beautifully
executed cartonnage or painted plaster
case that covered his linen-wrapped body.
The use of cartonnage, resin-soaked strips
of linen material modeled around a mud-
and-straw core in the general shape of
the body, seems to have come into fashion in the twenty-second Dynasty.

Amen-Nakht's face is rendered in
golden tones with lapis lazuli blue details, the traditional colors of a god's face
in Egyptian mythology. He wears an
elaborate striped wig cover and an unusual amulet around his neck above the
huge broad collar and winged scarab
beetle on his chest. Below the collar, the
body is divided into four large registers.
The upper scene shows the deceased
being led by the gods Thoth and Horus
to an offering table filled with jars and
foodstuffs. Behind the table stands the
great god Osiris, lord of the Underworld,
with his sisters, Nephthys and Isis. As the
most important register in the series, a
great amount of detail was lavished on it.
The second and third registers are filled
with protective fetishes and numerous
gods. The fourth register indicates that
the deceased has passed the tests of piety
and purity and has been accepted into the
afterlife by Osiris. Amen-Nakht kneels on
a small raised dais and is anointed by the
gods Horus and Anubis with water flowing from two large *hes*-vases.

The tops of the head and feet are
protected by winged scarabs, while the
ankh-sign and *weser*-staff, symbols of life
and authority respectively, encircle the
base of the cartonnage around the feet.

Winged Genius, 885–859 B.C.
Assyrian, Nimrud
Alabaster
59½ x 35¼ in. (151.1 x 89.5 cm.)
Purchase 186:1925

The Assyrian king Ashurnasirpal II
(885–859 B.C.) ruled from the palace at
Nimrud, one of the three great capitals
of his empire. The city was rebuilt after
883 B.C. with the labor of skilled craftsmen
brought in from territories conquered by
Ashurnasirpal's armies. Massive walls
were erected to house the increasing
wealth and protect the numerous royal
residences, temples, and administrative
offices of Nimrud. The colossal statues of
man-headed bulls that guarded the gates

served to humble visitors. Endless friezes
depicted conquests and votive scenes
with bird-headed beings who exalted the
power of the king.

The St. Louis relief is a portion of
the wall decoration that lined one of the
rooms of the Nimrud Palace. A winged
genius performs the ritual fertilization of
the date palm, a symbolic representation
of the king's divine connection and ability
to provide for his subjects. The cunei-
form inscription carved over the surface
provides a written description of the
action played out in the bold image.

Amphora, c.530 B.C.
Greek, Attic
Attributed to the Antimenes Painter
Ceramic
Height: 15¼ in. (38.8 cm.)
Purchase 39:1921

The primary scene on this elegant black-figure amphora depicts the Greek hero Herakles and the god Apollo engaged in combat for the Delphic tripod. Flanking the pair are the goddesses Artemis and Athena, who witness the battle. A circle of palmettes around the neck and base of the amphora, punctuated by a meander pattern, completes the decorative motif and enhances the figural scene.

During the Heroic Age of Greek mythology, one function of the sanctuary of Delphi was to cleanse wrongdoers of guilt. Herakles traveled to the site one day to purify himself, but was abruptly barred entry by Apollo. In a fit of rage, Herakles retaliated by removing the oracle's tripod, a necessary ritual object. Apollo intervened, and the fight began.

The black-figure process was perfected in the sixth century B.C. This decorative technique consisted of applying more finely sifted clay or slip to the body of a vessel. The object was fired in a reducing atmosphere, one without oxygen, and the surface turned black. At precisely the right time, oxygen was reintroduced into the kiln and the clay body became orange once again. The denser slip, however, remained black. Facial elements and other details were incised onto the surface with a sharp point before firing took place. Sometimes red and white were used to highlight the clay's natural rich orange, resulting in the high contrast of colors so sought after by Greek vase painters.

Grave Stele of Kallistrate, c.400 B.C.
Greek, Attic
Marble
32⅝ x 26¾ in. (83 x 68 cm.)
Purchase 4:1933

Grave reliefs of the Classical period usually showed a group of figures, with the deceased holding a prized possession or clasping the hand of a loved one. As on other large and important contemporary monuments, the name of the deceased was cut into the stele: "Kallistrate" appears on the architrave directly over the figure's head. Above that is summarily scratched the name "Kallisthenes Paiania," most likely identifying the father of the deceased. The woman's features are idealized, as she gazes beyond the things of this world.

Infant Herakles, 1st century B.C.
Greek
Black bronze with silver inlay
Height: 24¾ in. (62.8 cm.)
Purchase 36:1926

The solid stance, aggressive demeanor, and out-thrust powerful arm of this infant suggest that the figure is a representation of the hero Herakles. Although baby fat is apparent, the mature treatment of the face and the playful yet deadly grasp have been used to identify the child who gleefully strangled the snakes sent by Zeus' wife Hera to kill him while he slept in his nursery. Great attention has been given to the realistic rendering of anatomical features, muscular folds, and intricately carved curls that surround the rotund face.

The artificial darkening of the sculpture's surface is an impressive and rare example of so-called "Egyptian black-bronze" metalworking. This technique, favored in ancient Alexandria, was popular during the Hellenistic period.

Running Artemis

Greek, Hellenistic
Probably a 1st-century A.D. copy of a
4th-century B.C. prototype
Marble
Height: 28¾ in. (73 cm.)
Purchase 41:1924

Greek artists often portrayed the goddess
Artemis, sister of Apollo, in the guise of a
huntress. Great energy is apparent in this
running figure whose chest is bound by a
girdle which originally secured a quiver.
She probably held a bow in one hand
and was accompanied by a hunting dog.

A sheer garment reveals the goddess's
soft body, recalling the "wet drapery"
style popular in Hellenistic sculpture.
The drapery clings to the body yet swirls
about in deep folds and billowing trails,
highlighting a figure in animated, exaggerated movement. It is a fine copy of
the fourth-century B.C. Greek style,
which shows the sculptor's consummate
skill in creating fully revealed figures
beneath virtually transparent drapery.

Head of Domitia, c.80 A.D.
Roman, Flavian
Marble
Height: 11⅞ in. (30.2 cm.)
Purchase 22:1984

Funerary Bust of Priest Yedibel, 139 A.D.
Syrian, Palmyra
Calcitic marble
Height: 19⅞ in. (50.5 cm.)
Gift of Martha I. Love 24:1960

This portrait of the emperor Domitian's wife is typical of work from the Flavian Dynasty (A.D. 69–98), a period characterized by ornate and flamboyant art as well as ambitious building programs. The Colosseum was erected during this time, and it was Domitian who built the first palace complex on the Palatine Hill, where a succession of Roman emperors would live for nearly 200 years.

Domitia's personality manages to penetrate the smooth, otherwise idealistic features common to Roman Imperial sculpture. The small face peering out from the elaborate coiffure is subtly modeled; the banana curls illustrate the characteristic hairstyle of the era's female elite. Domitia was married to one of the most neurotic Roman emperors, and one imagines a will of iron beneath her beautifully formed visage.

Ancient Roman styles varied with time. In the wealthy provincial city of Palmyra, Syria, for example, tall free-standing monuments gave way to tomb towers and crypts similar to modern mausolea. During the first and second centuries, the surface area depicting a full figure was abbreviated to shorter cap stones with elaborate busts. These richly carved portraits in softer marbles or creamy limestone allowed patrons to be depicted in flowing garments, detailed hairstyles, and costly jewelry.

Yedibel's portrait is a striking example of this later canonical style. The rigidly frontal form of a young man is carved in deep relief. The cylindrical cap, known as a modius, denotes his priesthood, and the brooch that pins his tunic was probably originally inlaid with glass to suggest expensive jewelry.

Head of a Man, ~~4th century~~
~~Roman~~
Marble
Height: 9 in. (23 cm.)
Purchase: Gift of Mr. and Mrs. Lester
A. Crancer, Jr. in honor of Sidney
Goldstein; Museum Purchase, by
exchange 18:1988

Early Roman portraiture reproduced the
outward appearance of the sitter, a trend
that continued into the third century,
when the style changed irrevocably. The
mapping of exterior contours remained,
but a concentration on spirit and inner
strength became equally important. The
sitter's gaze was turned inward, no longer
confronting the viewer with imperial
certainty and power.

This head is a haunting fourth-
century portrait. The plastic modeling
of the third century has given way to a
flattened, almost ethereal façade. Some
scholars have suggested that many of
these later portraits were re-cut from
earlier heads, and that this piece may be
an example of that. Unlike early fourth-
century portraits which look up and out
for strength from beyond, our portrait
seems unfocused, lost in vacuous inner
contemplation, and unaware of the
viewer.

Head of a Bearded Man, C.200 A.D.
Roman
Marble
Height: 12½ in. (31.8 cm.)
Purchase: Museum Shop Fund, Funds
given by the Arthur and Helen Baer
Charitable Foundation, Mr. Christian
B. Peper, Sr., and Donors to the 1984
Annual Appeal; and Museum Purchase,
J. Lionberger Davis, Friends Fund, and
Mrs. Dora Gilula, by exchange 108:1989

The third century was a time of significant change in the Roman Empire. The
age of the soldier emperors began with
Septimius Severus, proclaimed emperor
by his troops in 193 A.D. A native of Leptis Magna in Africa, Septimius Severus
brought to Leptis the best architects and
sculptors of the time.

This over-life-size portrait of an aris-
tocratic Roman may have been carved by
a sculptor trained in the Greek tradition.
The subtle modeling of the brow, cheeks,
and slightly pursed mouth is extraordinary. The treatment of the finely detailed
beard and moustache contrasts with the
heavy, thick locks of hair. The sideward
glance suggests the portrait is not merely
a physiological map; there is apprehen-
sion in the gaze that avoids our eyes.

Plate, 9th–10th century
Iranian, Nishapur or Samarkand
Glazed slip-painted earthenware
Diameter: 14⅝ in. (37.2 cm.)
Purchase 283:1951

The Islamic mandate against "graven images" in art gave rise to a wonderful assortment of decorative motifs. The use of ornamental calligraphy was widespread, not only in manuscripts and tile surfaces but on metalwork and ceramic vessels as well. The bold and sure-handed inscription on this plate, which enlivens the rim with a rhythmic balance, decrees that "Planning before work protects you from regret."

The piece is one of an existing group of plates that similarly caution the reader to be assiduous, careful, and virtuous, thus comprising an almanac-like collection. Some scholars argue that these ceramics were made for a humble clientele, while others suggest that such aphorisms may have been admonitions directed at the wealthy middle class.

Sword Hilt, 13th century
Indian Sultanate Period or
Persian, Seljuk
Gold
3½ x 4⅞ in. (8.9 x 12.4 cm.)
Purchase 45:1924

This gold sword hilt is elaborately engraved with panels of scrollwork around the guard and a band of inscription circling the lower socket. Intricately carved lion heads adorn the ends of the guard, and both sockets are ringed with finely worked gold rope.

A complete translation of the inscription is hindered by the presence of a join over a key character. However, the text can be deciphered as "The exalted Lord, the greatest Khagan, the patriot (?), Sun of the State and the Faith, Succor of Islam and the Muslims, Greatest (warrior for the Faith? – Ghaz [i]?) (Bek Ilgham)."

Tankard or Jug (Minai ware),

13th century
Persian, Rayy
Glazed ceramic
Height: 5¼ in. (13.3 cm.)
Purchase: W.K. Bixby Oriental Art Fund
163:1952

During the twelfth and thirteenth centuries, the Persian city of Rayy was an important political, economic, and cultural center. It produced a variety of pottery, of which the most costly were called Minai wares. These thin-walled vessels were first glazed with an ivory or white ground, although some have a turquoise or blue underglaze. They are usually embellished with figural decoration not unlike contemporary manuscript painting.

Typically, Minai vessels were adorned with figures, horsemen, or banquet scenes outlined in red or black. Five sphinxes circle the shoulder of this vessel, with a man at one end of the procession and a vine at the other. The Kufic inscription which runs down the handle may be trying to quote a phrase such as "glory, prosperity (or good luck) and..." but letters are missing and the last characters are nonsensical. The decorator was probably illiterate and attempting to copy an inscription seen on another vessel.

Basin, 13th–14th century

Egyptian, Islamic, Mamluk
Brass with silver and niello inlay
Diameter: 21⅞ in. (55.6 cm.)
Purchase 50:1927

Patronage of urban structures and calligraphy reached new heights of refinement under the Mamluks in Egypt. This basin is an example of the portable objects crafted during the period that were often heavily adorned with sumptuous Kufic inscriptions.

The vessel, intended for personal ablutions, presents a rich and complex composition of epigraphy and ornament. The Kufic calligraphy is known as *thuluth,* used for architecture and large objects. It identifies the original owner of the basin as a Mamluk officer of the highest class:

The high authority, the lordly, the great amir,
the conqueror, the holy warrior, the defender,
the protector of frontiers, the fortified by God,
(The officer of) Al-Malik al-Nasir.

A similar inscription is found on the interior. Although there is no indication of who the vessel's maker or patron was, a later owner inscribed under the rim: "Made for our Lord al-'Imad."

Door Knocker, c.1290 A.D.
Egyptian or Syrian, Islamic, Mamluk
Brass with silver and niello
Length: 8⅜ in. (21.3 cm.)
Purchase 40:1926

Door knockers often were affixed to
monumental portals in the mosques and
royal residences of fourteenth-century
Egypt. This piece once adorned the door
of Qalawun, an important sultan who
maintained a complex of palaces in Cairo.

    The starlike pattern of the hammer is
offset by a series of beads that ring the
disk-plate. Silver inlay adorns both the
hammer, decorated with arabesques, and
the disk face containing the inscription.

Variant Star Rug, 16th century
Turkish, western Anatolia, Ushak
Wool
124 x 90 in. (315 x 228.6 cm.)
Gift of James F. Ballard 98:1929

Beginning in the fifteenth century, the
western Anatolian town of Ushak was
known for its large medallion carpets.
Such rugs get their name from the large
star-shaped medallions which are their
principal decorative elements. These
designs seem to have become popular
after the Ottomans sacked the Persian
city of Tabriz in 1514 and brought its
artists to the Anatolian court. Star Ushak
rugs were valued not only in the East but
also in Europe, where they are illustrated
in paintings as early as 1534.

    The richness of color and design
retained in this 400-year-old rug is dazzling. Although the deep-blue medallion
on a brilliant red ground is characteristic
of many Ushak works, the carpet is
unique in composition and condition.
While most rugs this age are worn to
their foundation, this has a full pile and
splendid hues. The scattered floral elements and the palmette and arabesque
borders are known in other rugs of this
type.

Doors, 16th–17th century
Spanish, Hispano-Moresque, said to be
from Toledo
Wood, gilt, iron, and paint
179⅛ x 106 in. (455 x 269.2 cm.)
Purchase 81:1937

These rare and well-preserved doors
represent an Islamic architectural decoration style popular for both religious and
secular use. They are thought to be from
the convent of Santa Isabel in Toledo,
where they would have led from an outdoor courtyard to an interior room.
Smaller doors, or posterns, were cut into
the lower part of both leaves for daily
use. Thus, it was not necessary to open
the entire door except on ceremonial
occasions.

The doors are of hollow-core construction, with an elaborate marquetry of
small inlaid wooden pieces that form a
star motif over the surface. The hollow-core technique allowed the enormous
structures to expand and contract, and
the marquetry surface could move during
such expansion and contraction without
suffering serious damage. The richly
painted decoration would have enhanced
an interior filled with equally elaborate
surfaces on walls and floors.

Asian Arts

Male Head, 2nd century A.D.
Indian, Mathura school, Kushan period
Sandstone
Height: 10½ in. (26.6 cm.)
Purchase: Museum Purchase and Friends
Fund 3:1970

Carved from the pink, mottled sikri
sandstone of Mathura, this strikingly
robust male head possesses the animated
qualities of portraiture. The head is comparable to older Indian sculpture in
which highly conventionalized features
are combined to suggest a lively individual personality. The intensely alert face is
composed of symmetrical, rhythmic
patterns produced by the abstracted
curvilinear forms of the brows, eyes,
moustache, and lips. The sense of antici-
pation within the features is further enhanced by the pneumatic tautness of the
full-fleshed cheeks and jaw.

Ardhanarishvara, 12th century
Indian, Tanjavar District, Tamil Nadu,
Chola Dynasty
Black granite
Height: 44¼ in. (112.5 cm.)
Purchase: Friends Fund 70:1962

The Hindu god Shiva is Ardhanarishvara, the Lord Whose Half is Woman.
Born from the mouth of Brahma, Shiva
emerged half male, half female. A symbol
of creation that paradoxically cannot
procreate, the androgynous Shiva is a
living biunity, a perfect self-fulfilled
whole. The physical differences of each
half of the figure are enhanced by male
attire on the proper right side and female
dress and jewelry on the left.

Shiva poses in a relaxed triply-flexed
stance. The piece is carved nearly in the
round; the openwork gives a finely pro-
portioned balance to the composition.
The elaborate crowned headdress and the
raised weapon and flower form extended
points which recall the *trisula*, the long-
handled trident carried by Shiva in his
ascetic Yogi appearance.

Axe, 3rd millenium B.C.
Chinese, Neolithic
Jade
Length: 9 in. (22.9 cm.)
Bequest of Leona J. Beckmann 20:1985

Excavations at the Chinese Neolithic site
of Dawen kou in Shantong province
have produced stone ornaments and
ceremonial implements of extraordinary
refinement, including bangles, blades,
and other objects. Finely wrought of
nephrite and jade-like stones, these objects had both ritual and utilitarian functions. The blade of this axe, made of a
cream-colored mottled stone, is perforat-
ed twice and bears a subtle design punctuated by aligned notches on one side.

Lijia, 11th century B.C.
Chinese, Shang Dynasty
(16th–11th century B.C.)
Bronze
Height: 18 in. (45.9 cm.)
Gift of J. Lionberger Davis 221:1950

The *lijia,* a vessel believed to have been
used to warm wine, efficiently exposed
liquids to the several heated faces of its
tri-lobed body. The decor on this bronze
is elegantly restrained, its monumental
expression conveyed by a bold shape,
smooth surface texture, and an almost
pneumatic tension in the swelling shoulders. A lengthy twenty-seven-character
inscription is cast on the outside surface
of the body, facing the handle.

   This *lijia* is said to have been discovered at Anyang, the site of a royal palace,
temple, and burial complex dating from
the later Shang Dynasty. Near the turn of
the century, the vessel entered the collection of the high Chinese court official
and art connoisseur Duanfang (1861–
1911), Viceroy of Tianjin.

■

Fanglei, 11th century B.C.
Chinese, Western Zhou Dynasty
(11th century–771 B.C.)
Bronze
Height: 24^{11}/$_{16}$ in. (62.7 cm.)
Purchase 2:1941

This wine container is a rectangular
variation of the round, vessel-type *lei* of
the Shang period (16th–11th century
B.C.). Unlike the more reserved and self-
contained presentation of the *lei*, the
surface of this early Zhou vessel bristles
with hooked flanges, spiked animal ant-
lers, and sharp angles. The multiplicity of
shapes and forms is further emphasized
in the large and unusual doubled animal
mask on the lower body, and in the
asymmetry of a single lug on only one
face of the vessel. A pictograph resem-
bling the ancient Chinese character for
water is cast on the inside neck of the
vessel and on the inside of the cover.

■

Hu, 9th century B.C.
Chinese, Western Zhou Dynasty
(11th century–771 B.C.)
Bronze
Height: 21^{1}/$_{8}$ in. (53.7 cm.)
Purchase 281:1948

Visual movement in Chinese bronze
designs was developed in the tenth
century B.C. with small bands of continuous meanders, or wave motifs. Ninth-
century artists took full advantage of
such rhythmic patterns on large-scale
bronzes such as the *hu*. Although similar
wine vessels dating from the late Western
Zhou period have been excavated from
Shenxi province, only a few bronzes
comparable in size and design to this *hu*
are in Western collections.

Shakyamuni Buddha, c.575 A.D.
Chinese, Northern Qi Dynasty
(550–577 A.D.)
Marble with traces of polychrome
Height: 76¼ in. (193.6 cm.)
Purchase 182:1919

Shakyamuni, born in approximately
563 B.C., was the historical Buddha of
India. A member of the royal Shakya
clan, he renounced his princely life when
he learned of suffering outside the palace
walls. Gaining enlightenment through
meditation, Shakyamuni devoted his life
to teaching others the path to salvation.
Buddhism later spread to China and
flourished there, fostering great temples,
scholastic centers, and richly ornamented
images of worship. Formal sculptures
were carved of white marble and overlaid
with gold and polychrome to portray the
Buddhist pantheon, including Shakyamuni dressed in monastic robes. The
inverted fan-shaped element and the
jewel carved between the feet are distin-
guishing features of this piece.

■

Bodhisattva, 8th century
Chinese, Tang Dynasty (618–906 A.D.)
Gilt bronze
Height: 11 in. (27.9 cm.)
Purchase 36:1933

Buddhism became a powerful cultural
force in eighth-century China as sacred
scriptures and icons were brought from
India to the great religious centers by
pilgrims and merchants. Imperial patronage, active theological studies, and the
introduction of new sects stimulated the
creation of extraordinary religious art.

    This sculpture of a *bodhisattva,* an
enlightened being of divine understanding and limitless powers, reflects the
opulence and vigor of high Tang culture.
The influence of the great Indian Gupta
style is revealed in the figure's broad
shoulders, tubular torso and limbs, and
clinging silks. Although several seated
bronze *bodhisattva* of the Tang period
exist, this work is distinctive for the solid, athletic quality of the body.

■

Covered Jar, 8th century
Chinese, Tang Dynasty (618–906 A.D.)
Earthenware with glaze
Height: 8¾ in. (22.3 cm.)
Purchase 18:1951

During the Tang Dynasty, ceramic wares
and figures were important funerary
goods in China. Made of dense earthenware, eighth-century pieces were wheel-
thrown to standard proportions. The
elegant, ample profile was usually covered with low-fire lead glazes. Amber,
green, and blue were the dominant colors, giving rise to the name *sancai,* three-
color wares. Examples with splashes of
blue on a white ground were somewhat
unusual. The costly cobalt blue, imported from Persia, was dabbed on in a seemingly random manner which, when fired,
resulted in a rare work of uncommonly
bold and expressive power.

■
Guanyin, 11th century
Chinese, Northern Song Dynasty
(960–1127 A.D.)
Wood with polychrome and gilt
Height: 39 in. (99.2 cm.)
Purchase 110:1947

Guanyin of Avalokiteshvara is a saintly
Buddhist figure of Indian origin. Known
in the West as the "Goddess of Mercy,"
Guanyin is actually a male *bodhisattva*,
an all-powerful enlightened being. Identifiable by the small seated Buddha in his
headdress, Guanyin remains in the world
to aid the salvation of all mortals.

The figure's calm, sensitive face and
informal but dynamic posture of royal
ease express compassion and strength. Its
ornate, princely attire is sculpted from
blocks of wood, carved, painted, and
gilded to convey the movement of gently
flowing silk and the sublime expression
of enlightenment. With the exception of
the right forearm and left hand, the
sculpture is remarkably free of later re-
pairs and reworking. The piece originally
sat on an artificial rocky ledge, part of an
elaborate and visually rich temple setting
in North China.

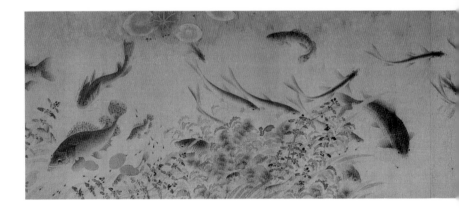

Fish Swimming Amid Falling Flowers,
12th century
Attributed to Liu Cai, Chinese,
late 11th–early 12th century
Song Dynasty (960–1279)
Handscroll: ink and color on silk
10½ x 99¼ in. (26.8 x 252.2 cm.)
Purchase: William K. Bixby Oriental Art
Purchase Fund 97:1926

Among Chinese painters of fish and their
watery environs, Liu Cai is celebrated for
capturing the vivid movement of aquatic
life in a detailed, realistic style characteristic of Song academic painting. In this
scroll, several varieties of fish are rendered in evenly gradated washes overlaid
with patterned textures of fine lines.

Soft and ephemeral, the waterplants are
"boneless," drawn in transparent colors
without lines.

The artist lived during the late
Northern Song dynasty (960–1127),
when imperial patronage of the arts was
most active. A highly esteemed painter
and poet, Liu Cai served the courts of
two emperors for more than four decades. Although this painting has no
signature or seals, its title and attribution
to Liu Cai have a recorded history of
more than 850 years. Treasured in the
imperial collections of four dynasties, the
scroll is a widely acclaimed masterwork
of the Song period. It was acquired by
The Saint Louis Art Museum from
Prince Jun, the father of Puyi, the last
emperor of China.

■

Wen Zhengming, Chinese, 1470–1559
Landscape in Rain, c.1540
Ming Dynasty (1368–1644)
Hanging scroll: ink on paper
28¼ x 12⅞ in. (71.8 x 32.7 cm.)
Purchase: Friends Fund 91:1986

Wen Zhengming was a founder of the influential Wu school of literati painting. A celebrated sixteenth-century poet, calligrapher, and painter, the artist was teacher and mentor to two generations of Ming period artists in the Suzhou region of southern China. In the theory and practice of literati art, however, Wen Zhengming was highly esteemed not only in China, but also in Japan.

Paintings like *Landscape in Rain* were based on personal experiences:

I remember painting this years ago.
It was a time under a single lamp in wind
and rain in a pine-wood cottage. The mud
and mire made the path slippery. I did
not go out, but instead sat waiting for
my servant to return with wine…

The memories surrounding the landscape are intimate and fresh as the artist writes his first inscription on the scroll many years after painting it. Upon seeing the work again ten years later, Wen Zhengming writes these poetic images:

The tree leaves whistle
[in the strong winds]
The sound rising and falling
The door is ajar
The mist rises to the clouds…

Landscape in Rain explores a special mode of Song academic painting that fascinated Wen Zhengming throughout his mature period of the 1540s and 1550s. Following the tenth-century master Li Cheng, Wen Zhengming created a repertoire of images which convey the bleakness and desolation of deep winter. But unlike the still, leafless trees and forlorn landscapes that characterize his other works in the Li Cheng manner, this scroll portrays nature in transformation, images constantly changing in wind and rain.

■

Gaoquan Xingdun (J: Kōsen Shōtōn),
Chinese, 1633–1695
Triptych: Cursive Script Calligraphy,
c.1678–1692
Edo period (1615–1868)
Set of three hanging scrolls: ink on paper
Each scroll: 52 x 14⅛ in. (132.1 x 36 cm.)
Purchase: Funds given by
Mrs. J. L. Johnson, Jr. 115:1988 a,b,c

Gaoquan Xingdun, an eminent Chinese
monk, poet, and calligrapher, began Zen
training in China at the age of eleven. In
1661 he emigrated to Japan to join the
assembly of his teacher Yinyuan Longqi
(1592–1673) at the newly established
Obaku Zen monastery of Manpukuji in
the environs of the capital city, Kyoto.

Gaoquan flourished in Japan. In 1678 he
founded the monastery Bukkokuji, becoming in 1692 Manpukuji's fifth abbot
and thus the fifth Patriarch of Obaku
Zen in Japan.

Obaku monks contributed widely to
the arts and sciences in Japan, and their
calligraphy was especially admired.
Gaoquan's triptych, executed during his
tenure as abbot of Bukkokuji, exemplifies
the Obaku style in one-line Buddhist
verses brushed in bold, large characters.
Gaoquan's dissemination of Obaku culture via prolific writings, ink paintings,
and works of calligraphy earned him the
attention of the Emperor, and, after his
death, the honorary title of National
Teacher.

Pair of Bowls, 18th century
Chinese, Qing Dynasty (1644–1911)
Porcelain with underglaze blue and
overglaze enamels
Mark: Yongzheng reign (1723–1735)
Diameter: 5¹⁵⁄₁₆ in. (15.1 cm.)
Diameter: 5⅞ in. (15 cm.)
Bequest of Samuel C. Davis
1031:1940.1,.2

Exuberant dragons and phoenixes have
long symbolized the vitality and power
of Chinese emperors and empresses. The
imperial emblems on these bowls are
finely rendered in brilliant enamels and
possess an exquisite jewel-like quality.
Known as *doucai* or "contending colors,"

porcelain ware designs of colored enamels
set over underglaze blue had been created
at the court kilns of Jingdezhen since the
fifteenth century. However, during the
reign of the Yongzheng Emperor, the
doucai method and the general character
of ceramic production reached a superlative point. The six-character mark
bounded by a double square on the foot
of each bowl further distinguishes the
quality of the vessels as befitting the
highest imperial order.

Gaozong, The Qianlong Emperor,
Chinese, reign 1736–1795
Poem, 18th century
Qing Dynasty (1644–1911)
Hanging scroll, gold ink on indigo-dyed
paper
63 x 29⅜ in. (159.8 x 74.5 cm.)
Purchase: Funds given by Mrs. Jack A.
Jacobs 80:1988

During the eighteenth century, imperial
arts in China reached superlative heights
under the patronage of the Qianlong
Emperor, Gaozong. As befitting the role
of patron, connoisseur, and collector
extraordinaire, the Emperor was also an
enthusiastic and prolific calligrapher and
poet.

This poem was written in Gaozong's
distinctive semi-cursive script. He employed opulent gold ink and rich indigo-
dyed paper normally reserved for small
handscrolls of Buddhist scripture. By
enlarging greatly both format and characters, he ingeniously expanded the play
between the secular poem and the brilliant gold and deep-blue materials so
intimately associated with sacred writings. For the sumptuous imperial brush,
Gaozong elevated his verse above the
profane with stunningly decorative effect.

Chaogua, late 19th century
Chinese, Qing Dynasty (1644–1911)
Silk satin weave with gold and silk
embroidery
Length: 42⅛ in. (107 cm.)
Gift of Mr. and Mrs. F. Russell Fetté in
memory of Helen Campbell Fetté
261:1986

The *chaogua* was a woman's sleeveless
outer vest worn over fuller imperial court
robes, and typically adorned with colored
designs against a blue-black ground. The
ensemble was completed by an elaborate
crown, the golden and bejeweled phoe-
nix coronet. During the Qing Dynasty,
the wives of high officials wore the dress
and emblems corresponding to their
husbands' positions. The court bureau-
cracy was broadly divided into civil and
military ranks. Primary insignia were the
dragon and the large embroidered badge
or "mandarin square," bearing a bird
for the civil grades and a beast for the
military.

The design of this *chaogua,* three
imperial dragons, two ascending in front
and one large rampant beast in back, was
worn by wives of dukes, lesser nobles,
and civil officials down to the seventh
grade. The mandarin duck which graces
the back of the vest is a symbol of felicity
and harmony, and signifies the seventh
civil rank.

Amida Nyorai, mid-13th century
Japanese, Kamakura period (1185–1333)
Lacquered wood with gold pigment, gilt,
and crystal insets
Height: 32½ in. (82.6 cm.)
Purchase 132:1966

Amida – or Amitabha – is Buddha, Lord
of the Western Paradise, the Pure Land
into which all souls of the faithful are
reborn. During the thirteenth century,
Japanese Buddhist temples were largely
supported by contributions from the
populace, and in response to its patronage, images of worship were made more
human, more approachable. Sculpted
from fine woods and overlaid with lac-
quer and gold, the images had such
descriptive details as eyes of sparkling
crystal. The hands were modeled on
tender gestures that would welcome the
saved to Heaven. Considered among the
finest of its type, *Amida Nyorai* is notable
for its construction, style, and decoration, which point to mid-thirteenth-
century Kyoto origins.

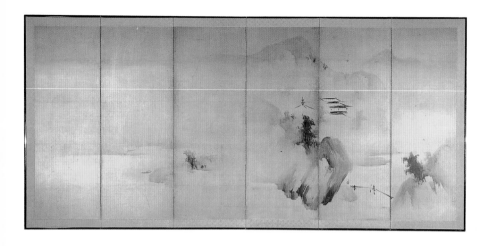

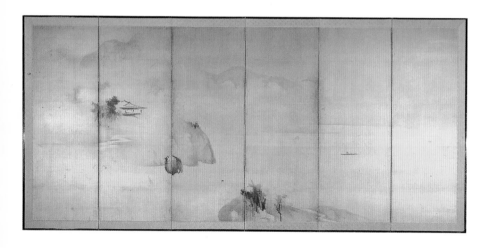

■

Kaihō Yūshō, Japanese, 1533–1615
Landscape, c.1602
Momoyama period (1573–1615)
Pair of six-panel screens: ink and gold on paper
Each panel: 62 x 139¼ in.
(157.7 x 353.8 cm.)
Purchase: Friends Fund 59:1962.1,.2

Born into a samurai (warrior class) family serving a regional clan, Kaihō Yūshō left home at a young age to train in one of the great Zen monasteries of the ancient capital, Kyoto. There he studied with Kanō Motonobu (1476–1559), one of the great painters of the day.

To evoke the image of a watery and mountainous scene, Yūshō drew on a long history of landscape painting in China and Japan. This tradition, called *suibokuga* in Japanese, relied primarily on effects obtained by saturating flexible animal-hair brushes with varying amounts of ink and water. Yūshō's monochromatic style recalls the work of Yujian, a medieval Chinese monk whose paintings were highly regarded in Japan. Yūshō can thus be placed in a long tradition in which the Buddhist notion of emptiness is expressed via the depiction of vast spaces, barren landscapes, secluded valleys, and distant mountain tops.

Masatsugu Kaigyokusai, Japanese,
c.1813–1892
Chago (Tea Measure), c.1870
Ivory with stain
Length: 6⅜ in. (16.1 cm.)
Signature: Kaigyokusai
Seals: Kaigyoku
Masatsugu no in
Purchase: Museum Shop Fund 75:1989

Kaigyokusai was an Osaka sculptor who
carved exquisite *netsuke* (toggles) of rare
woods, hornbill, shell, amber, and ivory,
all characterized by clarity of form and
expression. Because of his personal
wealth, the artist was free to use the
choicest materials for his *netsuke* and
larger works. He favored *tokata,* a lus-
trous ivory from Southeast Asia.

   The sumptuous quality and sophisti-
cation of this tea measure suggest that
it was made expressly for *senchado,* the
steeped tea ceremony. As in all of
Kaigyokusai's work, the design is
thoughtful; here it reflects the artist's
own deep understanding of tea.

Aoki Mokubei, Japanese, 1767–1833
Kyusu, datable to autumn of 1832
Edo period (1615–1868)
Stoneware with molded inscription
Height: 3¹⁵/₁₆ in. (10 cm.)
Purchase: William K. Bixby Oriental Art
Purchase Fund 126:1985

Although Mokubei is known as one of
the finest painters of the late Edo period,
he first attained fame as a potter of tea
wares. His *kyusu* or small teapots fully
expressed the literati values of simplicity
and scholarship that were so closely associated with *sencha,* steeped tea.

   This *kyusu* was one of a hundred such
teapots created by Mokubei in 1832 for a
large tea gathering to be held at Kitano
Shrine in the spring of the following
year. Mokubei died several days after the
last firing. This is one of a few remaining
teapots from the original one hundred.

Hine Taizan, Japanese, 1813–1869
Spring Woods, Passing Rain, 1856
Hanging scroll: ink and light color on
paper
76 x 37 in. (193 x 94 cm.)
Purchase: Museum Shop Fund 31:1985

Chinese literati-style painting appealed
to Japanese scholars, samurai, and merchants, who studied printed painting
manuals and copied scrolls imported
from China. Hine Taizan was one such
assiduous student, and the result of his
efforts is evident in *Spring Woods, Passing
Rain,* one of the most important works
he completed in his middle years. The
landscape in clearing rain was painted on
an exceptionally large single sheet of
imported Chinese paper, which bears a
repeated watermark of confronting dragons with a flaming jewel and rows of
lozenges down the sides. In yet another
link with China's great artistic traditions,
the scroll's composition and brushwork
evoke the paintings of the Chinese Wu
school master Shen Zhou (1427–1509),
whose style Taizan emulated throughout
his life.

Nukina Kaiokū, Japanese, 1778–1863
Cursive Script Calligraphy, 1850
Edo period (1615–1868)
Pair of six-panel screens: ink on paper
Each panel: 50¼ x 20⅜ in.
(127.6 x 51.6 cm.)
Purchase: Funds given by Mrs. Florence
Morris Forbes 181:1987.1,.2

The calligrapher Nukina Kaiokū came
from a provincial samurai (warrior class)
family. His early childhood education
featured training in the martial arts,
notably archery. A strong artistic inclina-
tion, however, led him as a young man
to travel in search of teachers versed in
calligraphy, painting, and Chinese literature and philosophy. In the last years of
his life, Kaiokū epitomized the erudite
Confucian scholar. He was a respected
authority on Chinese culture at a time

when Japan was about to experience a
tide of cultural influence from the West.

A master calligrapher, Kaiokū chose
for this pair of six-fold screens two classical Chinese poems, written in a script
style known as *sōsho,* "grass"or "cursive,"
for the vigor and freedom of the brush.
Intended to enliven an interior setting,
Kaiokū's effective magnification of ancient Chinese compositions onto the
large-screen format of the traditional
Japanese screen reflects the assertive
mastery of the artist in his maturity, and
records for posterity his assiduous commitment to Chinese traditions.

Sakai Hōitsu, Japanese, 1761–1828
Fans and Stream, 1820–1828
Edo period (1615–1868)
Fusuma mounted as a pair of two-panel
screens: ink, color, gold, and silver on
silk
Each panel: 67 x 35¼ in. (170.1 x 89.5 cm.)
Purchase: Friends Fund 140:1987 a,b

The general theme of *Fans and Stream*
can be traced to the Muromachi period
(1333–1573), when painted fans were past-
ed onto screens as decorations. In the
Edo period, the great Rimpa-style artists
Tawaraya Sōtatsu (seventeenth-century)
and Ogata Kōrin (1658–1716) enriched
the painting of multiple fans with bold,
innovative compositions, and infused
their works with distinctively Japanese
motifs. Sakai Hōitsu, an ardent admirer
of Kōrin, later revived Rimpa, merging
the highly decorative style with his own
genius for design.

Hōitsu originally conceived this
painting as decoration on *fusuma,* sliding
room partitions, with thirty fans rendered directly on the silk of four panels.
Unlike other works of the "folding fans
and flowing stream" theme, in which the
fans appear to float in waves, the artist
arranged his fans as if tossed into the air

in a "scattered" manner. The four seasons
are marked by native Japanese plants,
from the prunus buds of early spring to
winter's snow-covered cypress. Throughout the work, Hōitsu painted many of
Rimpa's most famous artistic and literary
motifs, including the waves at Matsushi-
ma, Uji Bridge, Mount Fuji, and the
irises at the Eight-planked Bridge.

Matazō Kayama, Japanese, born 1927
Tanabata (Star Festival), 1968
Single six-panel screen: ink, color, gold,
and silver on silk
Each panel: 65½ x 24⅛ in.
(166.3 x 61.3 cm.)
Gift of Mr. and Mrs. Matazō Kayama,
The Japan America Society of St. Louis,
and Dr. J. Peggy Adeboi 150:1987

Tanabata depicts the Milky Way from
the ancient Chinese and Japanese ro-
mance of two stars, the Weaving Princess
(Vega) and the Herdsman (Altair).
According to legend, the lovers were
banished to separate constellations in
Heaven and allowed to meet but once a
year, on the seventh night of the seventh
month, joined by the Milky Way. The

Man'yōshū, an anthology of early
Japanese literature, records their annual
meeting in a poem:

*... This evening when the autumn wind
arises,*
*Swaying the pennoned reeds, stalk and
blade,*
He in his red boat, many-oared
And gaily trimmed, bow and stern
*Buffeting the white waves of the Heavenly
River*
And crossing the swift and swirling waters,
Will come rowing – the lone Star-man...

In *Tanabata,* the galaxy is depicted
as a brilliant stretch of silver sprinkled
across a jagged ground of deep blue.
Slender bamboo in pale ink and silver
washes over a sparkling section of rich
gold bounded by billowing silvery waves;

46

a luminous crescent moon lies cradled in the undulating metallic lines. In Japanese lore, the moon is believed to reflect the image of a loved one who is far away. A rocky shore of light-blue pebbled aggregate is startlingly juxtaposed with patches of deep molten red and gold-dusted green.

Matazō Kayama is a leading artist of Nihonga, a modern Japanese style of painting. Although it is distinct from traditional art forms, Nihonga's themes, materials, formats, and styles allude to Japan's artistic past. In *Tanabata*, this is evident in the placement of ragged-edged colors and textures, which recalls *tsugigami*, patched decorated papers of various colors used for writing poetry in twelfth-century Japan.

Arts of the Americas, Africa, and Oceania

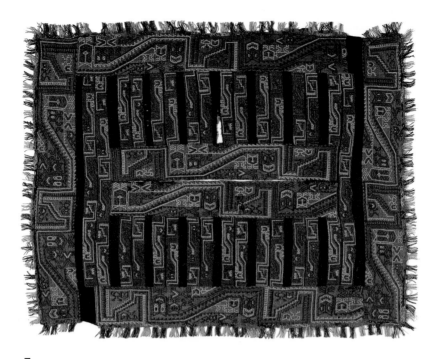

Poncho, 300–100 B.C.
Peruvian, South Coast, late Paracas culture
Wool embroidery on cotton
30 x 23⅝ in. (76 x 60 cm.)
Purchase 24:1956

Peruvian textiles of Pre-Columbian times are highly regarded for their extraordinary technique, color range, and complex design. In that elite group is this small poncho, one of many garments that would have been placed on the mummified remains of its owner. A skirt (mantle) and head strap also in the Museum's collection would have completed the costume dress for the deceased in his or her afterlife.

This weaving, which was created on a back-strap loom, consists of a solid cotton foundation with wool embroidery. As most New World cultures of the period, the Paracas venerated the cat. The poncho's geometric designs feature feline figures, most likely jaguars, with stepped-fret tails, and smaller cats in profile. The scalloped bodies of the cats suggest raised hair, which, considered with the wide-open mouths and stares of several of the animals, implies a fearful expression. Their stiffening stances may be intended to symbolically protect their owner from danger.

■
Head, 600–900
Mexican, Yucatán peninsula, Maya
culture
Lime stucco with blue-green and red
pigment
Height: 12¼ in. (31 cm.)
Gift of Morton D. May 150:1979

Figural sculpture often adorned the
façades of Maya temples and government
buildings during the classic period. This
object and five other such works in the
Museum's collection were found together
in the southern Yucatán peninsula. They
all were originally attached to façades by
tenons at the back. The pieces' individu-
alized expressions and heightened realism
indicate that the Maya used this kind of
sculpture as true portraiture, depicting
members of ruling dynasties.

This well-preserved head is most
likely the portrait of an aging ruler, as
suggested by his protruding cheekbones,
receding and toothless mouth, bulging

eyes, and long curving nose. The extended eyes indicate that the individual may
have suffered from goiter disease.

Viewed from a 180-degree perspective, this work of art is enlivened by the
play of planar edges and changing shadows which emerge upon approaching the
sculpture or moving around it. Such
visual sensations were intended by the
artist, who understood well the affective
power of shadow and line in relation to
the changing perspective of the viewer.

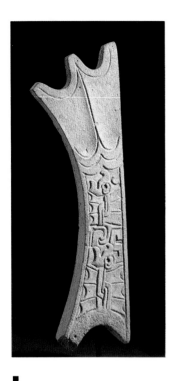

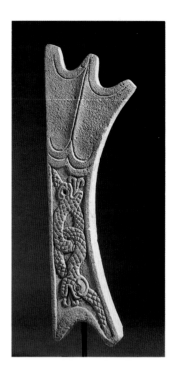

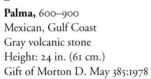

■
Palma, 600–900
Mexican, Gulf Coast
Gray volcanic stone
Height: 24 in. (61 cm.)
Gift of Morton D. May 385:1978

Palmas were associated with a ritual ball-game that was widespread in the Pre-Columbian world. Gambling and human sacrifice were important aspects of the game which, if successfully played, affirmed political power and good relations with the gods; production of maize depended on the latter. This stone sculpture most likely represents a wicker accoutrement which would have been placed on a player's U-shaped belt, extending from the front waist to the chest.

The soaring quality of this exceptional work of art results from its feather or bat-wing shape. Two bats carved in relief on one side echo the wing motif; moreover, the animals' wing sections repeat the general shape of the object. On the opposite side, intertwining snakes in relief complete the carving. Their interlocking tails probably depict the act of reproduction, underscoring the fertility aspect of the ball game and its rejuvenating function.

■
Old Man Leaning on a Staff, c.1200
Mexican, Gulf Coast, Huastec culture
Sandstone
Height: 22⅝ in. (57.5 cm.)
Gift of Morton D. May 361:1978

The Huastec people of northern Veracruz, Mexico, are best known for slab-like, three-dimensional stone sculpture that incorporates dual imagery. The subtle contours of the fully fleshed side of this piece are juxtaposed with the intricately carved bones and joints of its skeletal counterpart, creating a figure whose life-death, youth-age contrast is typical of the art of Pre-Columbian cultures with a dualistic world view. This dualism is formally reiterated by the figure's gaze upward toward the sky and the countering staff which links it to the earth. The Aztecs, who conquered the Huastecs in the mid-fifteenth century, may have incorporated certain Gulf characteristics into their three-dimensional stone carvings, such as a slabular quality, richly incised patterns, and an overall sense of balance.

Jaguar Pectoral, 1200–1500
Mexican, Central Highland, Mixtec
culture
Stone and shell inlay on wood
Length: 6½ in. (16.5 cm.)
Gift of Morton D. May 163:1979

One of the most prevalent motifs in Pre-
Columbian art is the jaguar, an animal
venerated from Olmec times onward and
associated with kingship. In this pectoral,
the artist has emphasized eyes, claws, and
teeth to convey the power of the feline.

In terms of sculptural realism, the animal's muscular essence has been successfully captured with a massive rendering
of the neck and short, stocky body,
which is faceted with tiny pieces of green
turquoise to represent the skin pattern of
the jaguar. Collar and tongue are made
of coral, while the eye is black jet. Teeth
and claws of white shell complete the
mosaic.

Polychrome Plate, 1200–1500
Mexican, Mixtec culture
Earthenware
Diameter: 9 in. (23 cm.)
Purchase 85:1950

Mexico's Central Highland cultures began to develop their complex ceramic tradition as early as 1500 B.C. Ranging from organic to abstract and utilitarian shapes such as this, most earthenware was deposited in burials to accompany the deceased on their journey to the underworld.

This beautifully shaped and painted vessel is carefully organized in a concentric pattern, with a hieroglyph-like central motif surrounded by borders and abstract signs. The circle of designs isolated by the interior silver and the exterior burnt orange borders symbolizes the sky band. Mixtec day signs such as "flint knife," "reed," and "eagle" encircle the rim. The total composition suggests a sun pattern with a solid inner core, radiating energy in the striated borders.

Female Figure, 1300–1400
Mexican, Central Highland,
Aztec culture
Wood, pigment
Height: 20⅞ in. (53 cm.)
Gift of Morton D. May 381:1978

Rarely do collections of Pre-Columbian art from Mesoamerica include wood sculpture, due to poor preservation conditions underground. This unusual example may depict the Aztec goddess of the water, Chalchiuhtlicue, whose name means "She of the precious jade skirt."

Remaining black and blue pigments on the headdress and skirt indicate that the image was once completely painted. Originally, the central disc-shaped plaque which the figure holds may have been inlaid with shell and jade, or, more likely, pyrite or obsidian mirror. Mesoamerican goddesses often are associated with mirrors used for divination, since they were assumed to be capable of seeing the future in the mirror's smooth, reflective surface.

Unlike the more naturalistic style of Maya sculpture, this object exhibits a rather hieratic and stiff style, emphasizing the frontal view. The vertically oriented figure is bisected proportionally by horizontal lines sustained by the plane of the head, hairline, shoulders, and the skirt's bottom edge.

■

Double-Chambered Whistling Vessel,
1400–1532
Peruvian, Central Coast, late Chancay
culture
Cream-slipped earthenware
Height: 12 in. (30.5 cm.)
Gift of Morton D. May 370:1978

Hand-crafted ceramics comprise one of
the largest categories of Pre-Columbian
art to have survived. Peruvian examples
from the period usually feature complex
polychrome painted decoration. Yet in
this example the artist has concentrated
strictly on the form of the vessel and its
linear compositional devices, established
by the edges. The circular rims of the
two chambers are reinforced by the curve

of the strap connecting the spout with
the bird. The chambers rest lightly on
annular footed bases which repeat in a
perpendicular position the chambers'
disc rim shapes. The daringly tall spout
tapering on its ascent is counterbalanced
by the mass of the low-perched bird.

Vessels such as this were made to
whistle. When water was passed from
one chamber to the other, or when someone blew into the spout, the whistle
outlet on the chamber with the bird
emitted a piercing sound.

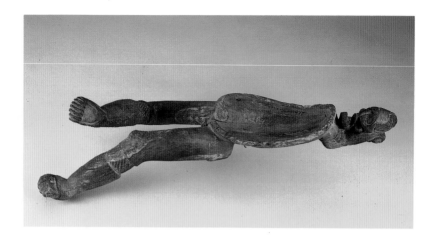

Effigy, 15th century
Caribbean, Dominican Republic,
Taíno people
Wood
Length: 24 in. (61 cm.)
Purchase: Friends Fund and Primitive
Arts Society Fund in honor of Morton
D. May 168:1981

This Zemi (Cemí) wood effigy from the
Dominican Republic belongs to an indigenous Pre-Columbian art tradition
that was widespread in the Caribbean.
Throughout the region, Zemi figures
were crafted with similar stylistic characteristics, including the emaciated treatment of the limbs. The frozen gaze of
the skull contrasts dramatically with the
animated and contorted positions of the
arms and legs. The underside of the
sculpture displays stylized ribs in a relief
of chevron patterns, further emphasizing
death.

This object was meant to be held for,
when placed in the hands, an easy grip is
achieved. It is likely that the effigy was
part of a ritual which may have involved
blood or human sacrifice. Such rites were
common on the mainland of Mexico,
where among the Maya and Toltec larger
stone images of similar shape served as
receptacles for human heart sacrifice. A
trough on the belly of those mainland
figures, recalled by the platform on this
effigy, would hold the offering.

■
Seed Jar, 1100–1300
American, New Mexico, Anasazi people
Earthenware, black and white pigment
Height: 10⅝ in. (27 cm.)
Gift of Mr. Edward Harris 175:1981

Tall shouldered vessels distinguish the
earthenware traditions of the ancient
Anasazi peoples of the American Southwest. Many were used for storing water.
This example, however, was most likely
used for storing seeds, since it lacks the
short-necked rim of the water vessels.

Fine brushes made of yucca fiber were
used to paint the complex geometric
design. The motifs include interlocking
frets in two bands with white lightning
patterns in between, highlighted by a
black background. The fret patterns are
composed of tiny white squares with dots
at the centers. These square shapes may
represent corn kernels, and the lightning
motifs may be symbolic of rain. Thus,
the water and seed subjects may make
reference to agriculture and fertility.

■
Bowl, 950–1150 A.D.
Mimbres people, New Mexico
Earthenware, pigment
Diameter: 9⅛ in. (23.1 cm.)
Purchase 113:1944

Mimbres people were part of a vast trade
network in the greater Southwest. Their
pottery tradition is principally a black-
on-white style and often depicts complex
representational scenes. Some of these are
multifigural and narrative, while others,
like the Museum's example, consist of
just one figure painted on the interior of
a bowl. While some finely painted bowls
were used in daily life, many were made
specifically for mortuary use.

The central, concave area of the
bowl's interior depicts a bat with out-
stretched wings. For Pueblo peoples, as
well as their Mesoamerican neighbors to
the south, this nocturnal animal is a
messenger of death and a creature who
accompanies the dead in the underworld.
On some Mimbres pots, the bat creature
appears as a human, with bat wings.
Here the bat is fully animal in form, but
has rabbit ears.

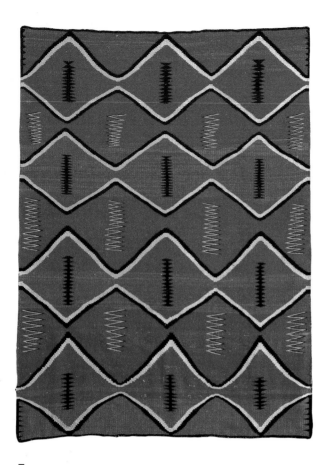

Blanket, 1865–1880
American, New Mexico, Navajo people
Wool with indigo and red aniline dye
49⅝ x 67⅜ in. (126 x 171 cm.)
Gift of Mrs. H.H. Bright 99:1975

Before the seventeenth century, the Navajo migrated from the upper plains of North America to the Spanish-occupied Southwest. They probably were taught the art of weaving by Pueblo neighbors who sought refuge in Navajo communities after their late seventeenth-century revolt against the Spanish.

This particular blanket was most likely woven during a transitional period (1868–1890) after the Navajo were incarcerated at Fort Sumner, near Bosque Redondo, New Mexico, and returned to

their homelands. While in captivity, they were influenced by the Mexican style of weaving that emphasized serrated edge designs as seen in this textile at the centers of the diamond shapes. The horizontal composition of the three rows of lozenges refers back to the earlier classical period (1650–1868), while the verticality of the serrated lines anticipates the transitional style. Classified as a *serape*, this textile would have been draped across the shoulders of its male owner or used as a sleeping blanket.

Maria Martinez, American,
San Ildefonso, Pueblo, 1881–1980
Plate, c.1943–1956
Slipped earthenware
Diameter: 14½ in. (37 cm.)
Gift of Mr. and Mrs. Charles Shucart in
memory of Margo Jester 526:1982

After several centuries of submission to
the colonial Spanish and Americans, the
quality of Pueblo pottery deteriorated
and production declined. At the turn of
the century, however, a revival spirit
emerged as a number of potters experimented with old and new designs and
forms. Maria Martinez began producing
pottery with her husband Julian in 1907.
After his death in 1943 she worked with
her daughter-in-law Santana Roybal,
with whom she created this masterpiece.

The plate dates to the period when
Maria preferred to work in the popular
black-on-black style. The feather motif at
the center is derived from similar motifs
on prehistoric Mimbres vessels found in
turn-of-the-century archaeological excavations.

Basket, 1900
American, California, Yokuts people
Attributed to Lucy Pete Fisher
Epicampes regens, sedge root, bracken
fern root
Diameter: 18¾ in. (47.5 cm.)
Purchase: The Western Art Purchase
Fund 40:1987

Known for the fine precision of their
work, the Yokuts were among the most
accomplished basket makers of California. This coiled basket combines
cloud patterns with swirling lightning
motifs that extend from the rim to the
base. The Yokuts, who occupied the
southern portion of the great San
Joaquín Valley, were dependent on the
rains for their livelihood, which accounts
for their artistic portrayals of clouds
and lightning, implying oncoming rain-
storms.

■

Potlatch Copper, c.1800–1850
North American, British Columbia,
Tsimshian or Kwakiutl people
Copper, paint
Height: 43½ in. (110.7 cm.)
Gift of Morton D. May 268:1982

Northwest Coast Natives developed a
unique painting and sculptural style that
relied on a continuous line and curvilinear composition to render images in a
stylized fashion. This large potlatch copper embodies that aesthetic tradition in
its depiction of a raven, the preeminent
character in Northwest Coast mythology.

On the front of the copper, two large
eyes loom from the upper portion, while
the beak, wing joints, and talons appear
beneath them. The back side shows the
raven painted in red in an ambiguous
style that combines profile and overview
perspectives, also typical of Northwest
Coast art.

Potlatch coppers were prestige items
often bearing a family crest and thus
legitimizing an individual's status in the
clan. Coppers could be passed on to
heirs, crafted to mark an important family event such as a birth or marriage, or
employed as a symbol of wealth and
conspicuous consumption when broken
into pieces and given away to members
of other clans.

Shaman Figure, 1880s
North American, British Columbia,
Haida people
Wood, paint
Length: 22 in. (56 cm.)
Purchase 132:1976

This superlative portrait of a shaman
(religious practictioner) reclining in
death is one of four such models known.
The others, in the American Museum of
Natural History, The British Museum,
and the Princeton Art Museum, are so
close in style to the Museum's example
that they are undoubtedly by the same
hand. All are attributed to the Haida
artist Gwaytihl, from the village of
Massett, a master carver who worked at
a time when commissions from white
patrons for models of the arts and cus-
toms of the past had replaced the monumental totem poles and other traditional
works done by previous generations of
artists.

The figure wears a fringed dance
skirt. His bent legs extend up through
the skirt, while his feet appear beneath
the skirt's fringes. The artist has represented the figure in an extreme state of
emaciation, indicated by the prominent
collarbone and ribs, the concave abdo-
men, and the sticklike arms and legs. The
face is carved with the skin taut against
the bones and the teeth revealed. As a
portrait of death and suffering, its compelling realism is of a kind seldom found
in Native American art.

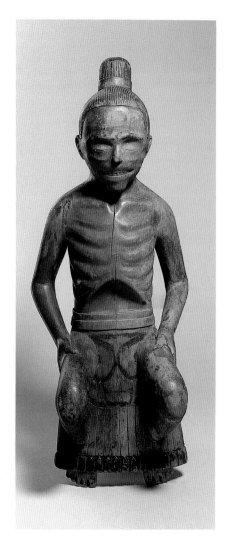

■

Head of an *Oba,* 15th–16th century
African, Nigeria, Benin
Bronze
Height: 8⅛ in. (20.8 cm.)
Purchase 12:1936

Bronze casting in the African Kingdom
of Benin reached a high level of virtuosity
by the fifteenth century. Artists were the
property of kings *(Oba),* who counted on
their talents to cast images that would
sustain the political authority of the royal
line. This sculpture is an example of the
early style of that tradition, characterized
by heightened realism. In ritual contexts,
the casting would have been placed on a
dais, and an elephant tusk carved in relief
with scenes from the life of the monarch
would have projected from the hole on
the top.

The elaborate coral-bead cap and
collar express the king's power. Coral was
considered the property of the divinity of
the ocean, and by extension, of his living
representative, the king. The combined
power of the spiritual undersea world
and the earthly domain controlled by the
Oba ensured the inviolability of the state.

Headrest, late 19th century
African, Zaire, Yaka people
Wood, copper
Length: 8⅝ in. (22 cm.)
Purchase 20:1942

The large leopard image and smaller relief carvings of animals on the annular base, including a bird at right, comprise the two parts of this articulately sculpted headrest. Copper nail heads on the leopard's face and traces of three similar heads may represent the animal's spots.

This headrest was kept in the sleeping room of a chief, who would place his head on the leopard's back; the use is substantiated by a dark patina. Often, packets of protective medicine called *musau* were attached to headrests to protect their royal owners from witchcraft. The chiefs themselves were believed to possess powers of witchcraft, and were able to transform themselves into leopards to punish offenders to their office, which often included witches. The leopard spirit empowered the chief; the bird images' aerial view and the quadruped animals' view in front and behind gave the chief omniscient vision even while he slept. Additionally, the bird may have been a symbolic messenger of the chief, for in African art birds frequently are associated with witchcraft.

Headdress, late 19th century
African, Nigeria, Eket people
Wood, basketry, black and white pigment
Height: 29½ in. (75 cm.)
Gift of Morton D. May 274:1972

This object combines woven art and
subtractive sculpture in the vigorously
expressionistic style of the Ibibio-related
peoples. The headpiece was most likely
worn by young male dancers of the
Ogbom secret society at masquerades
held in honor of the great earth goddess
Ala or Isong. To complete the costume,
a body suit of raffia or cloth would have
concealed the masquerader's identity.

The dramatically concave-cut facial
planes of cheeks and chin are countered
by the vigorous thrust of the quarter-
sphered forehead and echoed in the
curve of the nose. Three black triangular
forms pointing downward at the top of
the forehead, the base of the neck, and
on the carved pedestal determine the
vertical axis. The figure's posture suggests
downward movement and conveys a
sense of surefootedness. This stance contrasts with the flexed positions of arms
and legs, as if the figure were preparing
to spring. Such upward motion is echoed
in the arching black eyebrows and the
upswinging curve of the black design
painted at the back of the head. When
reviewed in profile, the sculpture emerges
as an image of opposing motions within
a highly integrated serpentine contour.

Reliquary Figure, 1880–1910
African, Gabon, Kota people
Wood, brass, copper, iron
Height: 24½ in. (62.2 cm.)
Purchase: Gift of the May Department
Stores, Mr. and Mrs. Alvin S. Novak,
Morton D. May, Ernest Anspach,
S. Thomas Alexander, S.Thomas
Alexander and Michael Roth, J. Lion-
berger Davis, Jerry O. Wilkerson, and
Bequest of Morton D. May, by exchange;
Museum Purchase and Friends Fund
23:1989

Sculpture such as this Kota figure was
eagerly sought by collectors at the turn
of the century, and to this day retains a
high value in the repertory of African art.
This type of figure inspired artists like
Picasso and Modigliani, both of whom
appreciated the highly abstract geome-
tries that African artists used to render
facial composition. The object derives
sculptural power from exploiting the
horizontal plane of the crescent-shaped
coiffure, the axis line established by the
slit eyes, and the suggested line between
the two side points of the lower lozenge.
The overall horizontal composition is
dramatically countered by the iron stria-
tions extending downward across the
cheeks from the corners of the eyes.

In context, this figure would have
been placed within an open bark container of ancestral bones with other similar objects, on a porch attached to a lineage house. Empowered by the bones,
such items protected the household from
outside danger and likewise insured its
prosperity. The arms akimbo gesture
implied by the figure's lozenge shape
cautions visitors to stop. The warning is
compounded by the shiny surface of the
brass appliqué, for amongst the Kota,
brightly reflecting objects are considered
dangerous.

Reliquary Figure, before 1910
African, Gabon, Fang people
Wood, iron, brass, palm oil
Height: 19⅜ in. (49.4 cm.)
Purchase 23:1942

At one time, these figure carvings *(bieri)*
of the Fang were placed on bark baskets
(nsuk) filled with the bones of ancestors.
The *nsuk* were in turn set within lineage
compounds, where they marshalled the
ancestors' spiritual power to ensure the
well-being of the living household.

The strictly imposed symmetry of
this sculpture, established by the central
axis running in a line down the center
of the forehead, through the nose, and
between the breasts, is a remarkable artistic device which divides the carving into
two opposing halves. Such a sculptural
contrast stands as a metaphor for the
nature of vitality, which the Fang view as
consisting of oppositions. Placement of
the infantile-shaped head and broad,
high forehead on a fully developed adult
body represents one set of opposites.
Taken as an ensemble, the smooth,
polished wood figure seen against the
lackluster of the bark container would
have created another set of opposites,
thus insuring vitality. The minimalist
treatment of the feet, legs, arms, and
chin suggests that the object was made
by the southern Fang.

■
Maternity Figure, middle 20th century
African, Yoruba people
Wood, indigo
Height: 16⅛ in. (41 cm.)
Purchase: Friends Fund 68:1989

One of the most powerful motifs of
Yoruba civilization is that of the mother
and child. Although this object suggests a
specific reference to the creative potential
of women, it communicates more generally the concept of *ashe,* which means to
create out of nothing. *Ashe,* the power to
bring about great things including each
new generation, sustains the vitality of
Yoruba culture.

In this singular masterpiece in the
Igbo Mina style of North Central Yoruba-
land, the artist has articulated body parts
and negative spaces in architectonic
terms realized through acute angles and
"V" shapes. The angle of the feet and
lower legs to the ground plane suggests

that although the figure is resting, she is
poised for action. The generosity of the
female, and by extension Mother Earth,
is indicated by the elongated breasts
which literally cascade into the waiting
infant's mouth. The dynamic qualities of
sculptural detail and mass are fitted into
an overall syntax of form which conveys
ashe, the power to create.

Blue, the color of the divine in Yoruba
cosmology, distinguishes the mother's
head and sinuous coiffure. The stylized
double-celt stool on which she sits suggests that she is supported by the god of
thunder, Shango. This sculpture was
most likely commissioned by a woman
to give thanks to Shango for her fertility.
Thus, the object may have been intended
for an altar dedicated to the deity.

Canoe Prow, c.1800
Polynesian, New Zealand, Maori people
Wood
Length: 21¼ in. (54 cm.)
Bequest of Morton D. May 1558:1983

The Maori, inhabitants of New Zealand
since the eleventh century, are a strongly
tribal people whose belief in ancestral
mythology is reflected in the treasured
wood, stone, and bone sculpture that is
their artistic trademark. Maori craftsmen
strive to incorporate authority, fear, and
power into their works while maintain-
ing distinct tribal styles. This prow, or
tauihu, once adorned a fishing canoe, its
riveted eyes and protruding tongue creating a fierce being who would ward off
evil and protect the canoe's occupants.

Ancestor Figure, early 19th century
Melanesian, New Guinea, Astrolabe Bay
Wood
Height: 51⅛ in. (130 cm.)
Gift of Morton D. May 43:1977

This rare figure sculpture is noteworthy
for its composition, particularly the manner in which the primary sculptural force
converges on a vertical line suggestive of
downward motion. The bird's beak and
the ancestor's elongated nose, extended
chin, plaited beard, and arms resting
firmly on hips all reinforce the downward
direction of the composition. The bird's
beak implanted in the cranium is a widespread motif in Melanesian artistic traditions. It is frequently associated with the
practice of head hunting.

Hook Figure, early 20th century
Melanesian, New Guinea, Middle Sepik
Wood
Height: 92⅛ in. (234 cm.)
Bequest of Morton D. May 1319:1983

This example of a hook figure was carved
by the Arambak people, dwellers of New
Guinea's Middle Sepik region along the
Karawari River. The spirit forces which
inhabited such power figures were con-
sulted by *shamans,* individuals who had
direct contact with the spiritual world, to
identify the right times for head-hunting
forays. The objects were kept in sacred
men's houses, away from the view of
women and children.

The linear, emaciated treatment of
the human figure is intended to convey
the idea of death. Although the ribs are
portrayed in profile, they are presented
frontally. Above the rib section is the
head, which may represent that of an
intended victim of the foray. Echoing
the curve of the ribs, the bird's head and
its projecting beak arch over the carved
head. In Middle Sepik cosmology, the
bird, specifically the cockatoo, is likened
to the headhunter in that it seeks the
fruit of trees. Tree stumps and limbs are
metaphorically bodies and limbs of men,
while the fruits are likened to human
heads. Thus, like birds, warriors in feather
dress hunt the fruit of humankind, the
head. In this magnificent and ominous
object, the bird's beak is poised as if to
pick to pieces the human head of the
carving.

Memorial Pole, 20th century
Melanesian, New Ireland, Malanggan
people
Wood, fiber, operculum with red, black,
and white pigment
Height: 94½ in. (240 cm.)
Gift of Morton D. May 60:1977

New Ireland peoples are renowned for
their intricate and complicated figure
carving. Sculptural images such as this
were crafted as memorials to the deceased, to ensure their safe passage to the
spirit world. Interlacing snake and bird-
like forms and lozenge-shaped masks
throughout the pole make it a superb
example of openwork carving. The up-
ward-moving composition is crowned
by a type of ancestral spirit mask whose
eyes of operculum stare imposingly at the
viewer. The artist has painted the individual animals and faces in different
colors in order to distinguish each one
in this complicated matrix of form.

Godstick, late 18th century
Polynesian, Hawaii
Wood
Height: 12 in. (30.5 cm.)
Bequest of Morton D. May 1532:1983

Though small in scale, this well-carved sculpture renders the various body masses in a monumental style by emphasizing the massive head, broad shoulders, and wide calves and feet. Such a representation is consistent both with ancestor worship and with the respect of the living for the deceased elders and their obvious physical and psychological strengths. The large scooped-out eyes and grimacing mouth reinforce the object's patriarchal quality. The head crest most likely represents a raffia woven crown, which high-status elders were entitled to wear. These figures were placed on the thatched roofs of sacred shrines or impaled in the ground for ceremonial functions.

Breastplate, early 19th century
Polynesian, Fiji, Rewa District, Viti Levu
Pearl shell, whale ivory, sennit
Diameter: 9 in. (23 cm.)
Bequest of Morton D. May 1557:1983

In Fijian tribal society, clothing and ornaments denoted status and prestige. Large breastplates of pearl shell and whale ivory were among the most impressive ornaments worn by powerful chiefs in battle and on important ceremonial occasions.

In this superb object, the ivory has been carefully split into seven plates, riveted together with ivory pegs, and inlaid with highly polished shell to create a dazzling convex ornament to hang around a chief's neck. The alternating circular and linear design elements, along with the juxtaposition of dark and light colors, create a formal artistic tension that is elegant in its simplicity.

European
Painting
and Sculpture

Workshop of Roger of Helmarshausen,
German
Crucifix Figure, c.1130
Bronze
Height: 7 in. (17.8 cm.)
Purchase 73:1949

The creator of this bronze figure of the
crucified Christ did not find his model in
nature. As a medieval artist, he looked
instead to other works of art, especially
liturgical furnishings, because he believed
that such precious objects possessed a
greater authority than the imperfect
forms found in the everyday world.
The model in this case was a group of
eleventh-century ivory carvings. Undis-
tracted by the confusion of nature, the
sculptor concentrated on the essential
elements of the figure, refining forms to
their simplest geometric equivalent.
Thus, the body of Christ is composed of
a sequence of smooth cylindrical and
spheroid shapes, incised with regularly
spaced lines to suggest the ribcage,
strands of hair, and other details. The
simplicity of these abstract forms imparts
to the piece a grandeur and solemnity
that belie its diminutive size. At the same
time, the sensitively modeled facial features bespeak the humanity of Christ and
his suffering, an aspect emphasized by the
bleeding wound scratched into the side
of the torso.

This sculpture is probably a product
of the workshop of Roger of Helmarshausen, an important and influential
artist who worked near the year 1100.
His name is known from a signed portable altar made for the Bishop of Pader-
born. Some scholars of medieval art see
the master's hand in this work, while
others assign it to an unknown follower.
In either case, this tiny figure is an outstanding example of both the technical
finesse of the bronze caster and the expressive power of a divine vision.

Enthroned Madonna and Child,
12th century
French, Auvergne
Polychromed wood
Height: 35⁹/₁₆ in. (90.4 cm.)
Purchase: Friends Fund 279:1952

One of the most interesting types of
Madonnas from the medieval period is
the "Throne of Wisdom" version, characterized by a seated, frontal Madonna who
in turn serves as a throne for her Son.
The name comes from the Latin *sedes
sapientiae,* a commonly used appellation
for the Virgin Mary which is taken from
the Book of Psalms and refers to Mary's
role as the vessel that bore the Son of
God. It is this role that is underscored in
"Throne of Wisdom" Madonnas, not the
Virgin's maternal relationship with her
Child.

In order to represent the Virgin as
vessel rather than mother, the artist who
created this wood sculpture chose particularly rigid poses. Mary's form repeats
the lines of the throne on which she
sits, and the flat plane of the Child's back
echoes that of His mother. He stares
straight ahead; there is no intimate play
between mother and Son.

This piece, originally polychromed,
is representative of Romanesque sculpture in a number of ways. Its anti-natur-
alistic treatment of the two figures, while
appropriate to the theme, is also typical
of French art of the eleventh and twelfth
centuries. The drapery folds that cascade
in relatively shallow waves across the
Virgin's shoulder and back are characteristic of this style as well. Although beautiful in themselves, their purpose is to
enhance and embellish the Madonna
rather than represent actual cloth whose
voluminous bulk could obscure the form
beneath.

Diptych with Scenes of Christ's Passion, 13th century
French
Ivory
8 x 6¾ in. (20.5 x 17.3 cm.)
Purchase 183:1928

Ivory, a precious and easily carved material, was a popular medium among medieval artists, since it allowed great detail and visual complexity. This work, a small devotional diptych, is derived from a form originally used by Roman and Byzantine emperors for tablets commemorative of imperial acts. The piece was probably used in private prayer and, like much of medieval sculpture, originally was painted.

Scenes of Christ's Passion, that is, the events immediately leading to his betrayal, arrest, and execution, were frequently depicted in small-scale objects of this sort. The diptych's narrative begins on the lower left, where Judas is tempted and then paid for betraying Christ, which he does in the third scene.

Judas hangs himself, Christ is arrested, and Pilate washes his hands. The story continues on the right of the second register, where Christ is tormented, bears His cross to Calvary, is crucified, and then is taken down from the cross, buried, and mourned. The second level ends with the scene of an angel telling the three Marys who come to the tomb that Christ has been resurrected. The upper register begins on the left, where Christ goes to purgatory to release those born before Him who were to be saved. This scene is unique in the diptych because it continues into a second compartment, where the hell-mouth consumes the damned. The final four scenes depict Christ's appearance to Mary Magdalene, the Virgin Mary with the disciples, the apostle Thomas verifying Christ's wounds, and the Ascension of Christ, represented by a hem and two dangling feet. All the scenes are contained in architectural compartments which recall the parts of a church and may indicate that the artist worked from an illuminated manuscript as a model.

Apocalyptic Scene, 1279–1285
Italian, Paduan school
Tempera and gold leaf on parchment
6¾ x 4¾ in. (17.3 x 12.1 cm.)
Purchase 117:1952

The most plentiful examples of medieval painting are contained in hand-painted religious books for liturgical and personal use, and include full-page illustrations as well as large initials that frame smaller images. This decorated initial, cut down from its original size, most likely accompanied a passage from the Book of Revelation, a work filled with vivid descriptions of the end of time, the apocalypse.

The setting includes a barren mountain and a religious structure. Two figures, perhaps angels, blow horns while a river of flame issues from the mouth of a dog-like creature on the right-hand side. Size relationships are grossly distorted, and nature's forms have been dramatically altered, resulting in a dramatic vision of time in which surface display and richly patterned forms take precedent over the details of the visual world.

The scene was executed on parchment using tempera paint, ground color suspended in egg yolk. The process of preparing parchment required scraping and beating an animal skin until it was thin and its surface smooth. A glue-mixture called sizing was then painted onto the page to ready it for the application of gold leaf. The gold was beaten into a very thin sheet, which was laid on to the vellum with a brush. The artist then burnished the gold with a tool, often a tooth attached to a handle, until it had a highly polished surface.

Madonna and Child, 14th century
French, Burgundy
Limestone
Height: 74⅝ in. (189.7 cm.)
Purchase 2:1930

Perhaps the single most frequent sculptural group of the later medieval period was the Virgin and Child. Representations of Mary appear in many types and forms, since she was the Queen of Heaven, the mother of Christ, an intercessor for prayers to God, an object of prayer herself, the patroness of many cities and guilds, the ideal of feminine virtue, and the model of the courtly lady.

During the thirteenth and fourteenth centuries, various regional French schools developed physical types of the Madonna and Child that served as models for the depiction of that theme. In eastern France, Madonnas with plump, wide faces wearing serious expressions predominated. Their bodies were heavy, and drapery was defined by relatively shallow folds that fell in even rhythms revealing the rather ample forms beneath. As exemplified by the St. Louis piece, this regional type of Madonna often incorporated elements of the courtly queen model that originated in Paris and the Ile-de-France, features such as a veil and crown. This figure's overall elegance, while not delicate, also derives from the Ile-de-France model; it is achieved through the long, curving sweep of the composition, from the fleur-de-lis crown down through the robe's gentle, supple folds.

Tomb Relief, 14th century
German, Odenwald region
Sandstone
68¾ x 40 x 6 in. (174.6 x 101.6 x 15.2 cm.)
Purchase 95:1932

European churches and monasteries were often repositories of sepulchral reliefs and sculptures created for wealthy families. The art works could be located within a family chapel, as this relief once was housed in Steinbach Abbey in the Odenwald region, not far from Frankfurt. The piece was displayed either on the floor or vertically upon a wall. It portrays a brother and sister, Elisabeth and Ulrich von Erbach, the children of Count Eberhardt Schenk von Erbach (d. 1377).

The tomb, carved in rather shallow relief, shows the tendency for elongation and the elegant lines typical of the Gothic style. Moreover, it is a good record of contemporary fashions, and was reproduced in a nineteenth-century treatise on the history of costume. The sister wears a long gown that fits tightly to the hip, with an off-the-shoulder neck and long tassels at the elbows. The brother's clothing is also close-fitting, with a tunic belted at the hip and tassels similar to his sister's.

The inscription surrounding the two figures is carved into a scroll that unfurls around the edges of the relief, ending in the center. Elisabeth stands upon a dog, a conventional symbol of fidelity, while Ulrich stands atop a lion, a familiar heraldic animal. Above their heads are family coats of arms.

Orcagna (Andrea di Cione), Italian,
c.1308–1368
Madonna and Child with Saints,
"The Sterbini Triptych," c.1345
Tempera and gold leaf on panel
16 x 17½ in. (40.7 x 44.5 cm.)
Purchase 51:1926

Orcagna was one of the most prominent
painters, sculptors, and architects of the
Florentine Trecento. In this richly
adorned triptych, at one time part of the
Sterbini collection in Italy, the Queen of
Heaven hovers within an almond-shaped
field of golden rays called a *mandorla.*
She is attended by six angels and a group
of saints including Peter, Paul, John
the Baptist, Francis of Assisi, and Mary
Magdalene.

Like many of his contemporaries,
Orcagna rejected the humanized naturalism of Giotto in favor of a style given to
flattened figures, strong contours, intense
colors, and unnatural space. Lest the
viewer be tempted to read recognizable
space into this work, the artist has asserted
the flatness of the picture surface through
beautifully punched borders that echo
the lines of the frame. Thus, Orcagna
presents a vision of the resplendent
Madonna enthroned in the heavenly
realm, holding before her the Son whose
incarnation promises salvation to the
believer.

St. Christopher, late 15th century
French, Burgundy
Limestone
Height: 31 in. (78.7 cm.)
Purchase: 3:1934

St. Christopher was one of the most
popular Catholic saints for personal
veneration and artistic representation.
The name means Christ-bearer, and
Christopher's fame stems from his having carried the Christ Child across a
deep and dangerous river. Tradition
maintained that Christopher, originally
named Reprobus, was a man of unusual
height who sought to serve the mightiest
ruler on earth. He was instructed by a
hermit to build a hut beside a particularly
treacherous river and, by ferrying people
across it, he could serve Christ, the
mightiest ruler. One night, a child asked
Christopher to carry him across. When
the man was barely able to carry the
child, Christopher asked why He was so
heavy. The child replied that He had

created the world and carried all its wor-
ries. After this experience, Christopher,
now a Christian, converted others to the
faith.

This limestone fragment is missing
the figure of the infant Christ normally
shown atop the saint's back. The staff, a
traditional attribute of the saint, is also
missing. Our piece came originally from
around Dijon, France, a thriving court
center in Burgundy between the thirteenth and fifteenth centuries. Burgun-
dian sculpture of the late fifteenth century is characterized by great attention to
naturalistic detail, as can be seen in the
treatment of the facial wrinkles and ring-
lets of hair. Most famous among the Bur-
gundian sculptors was Claus Sluter. Although it is unlikely that this piece is by
Sluter's hand, it was a product of that
same court circle that created some of the
greatest examples of late Gothic sculpture. The sensitivity of facial expression
and the sweeping form of the saint attest
to the skill of the sculptor.

Piero di Cosimo, Italian, 1462–1521
The Madonna and Child Enthroned with St. Peter and St. John the Baptist, St. Dominic, and St. Nicholas,
c.1485–1490
Tempera with oil glazes on panel
65½ x 44½ in. (166.4 x 113 cm.)
Purchase 1:1940

The Renaissance mastery of light and space is nowhere more in evidence than in this altarpiece. The painting is marked by richness of color, clarity of form, and engaging naturalness in the representation of light and shadow. It is in its original frame, which carries the coat of arms of its donor, a member of the prominent Pugliese family of Florence.

The Madonna holds the gesturing Christ Child in her lap. St. Peter, keys in hand, stands to the left embracing a kneeling Dominic, whom he presents to Mary. To the right, St. John the Baptist gestures toward Christ, whose mission he traditionally announces. St. Nicholas, identified by the three gold balls in his left hand, kneels at the right, gazing intently at Jesus.

The four attendant saints surround the Madonna to form a cohesive grouping. A work of this type, known as *sacra conversazione* (sacred conversation), departs from the older tradition which placed saints in individual compartments separated from the Madonna. The scenes in the smaller horizontal panels, called the *predella,* refer to the founding and mission of the Dominicans.

Tiziano Vecellio (Titian), Italian,
c.1488–1576
Ecce Homo, c.1570–1576
Oil on canvas
43 x 36½ in. (109.2 x 92.7 cm.)
Purchase 10:1936

Venetian art, which triumphed in the
latter part of the sixteenth century, was
noted for its bravura effects of richly
painted color. Titian's late works are
especially glorious examples of this
sumptuous technique, and *Ecce Homo*
was executed at the very end of the artist's
long career. Evidence of the brush is
found throughout the canvas, revealing
a dazzling assurance in the application
of paint and the evocation of texture
and surface. Working from a darkened
ground, the artist built up areas of lighter
tonality while retaining a hazy, veil-like
atmosphere appropriate to the theme.

Although unfinished, the painting
has great expressive power; it evokes a
sense of spiritual reverie and invites the
viewer to contemplate the suffering and
humiliation inflicted upon Christ. Originally charged with blasphemy by the
high priests of the Jewish Sanhedrin,
Christ was turned over to the Roman
governor Pontius Pilate, whose soldiers
taunted and mocked him for claiming
to be "King of the Jews." They crowned
him with thorns instead of gems and
presented him to the assembled mob,
declaring "Ecce Homo" (Behold the
Man); this was a perverse reference to
the words of John the Baptist, who had
originally preached the coming of the
Saviour.

Titian has placed Christ close to the
picture surface, flanked in a crowded
composition by a page on His right and
Pilate on His left. He is bleeding. His
inclined head and averted gaze are powerful devices to draw the viewer into the
painting.

Giovanni Angelo Montorsoli, Italian,
c.1507–1563
Reclining Pan, c.1535
Marble
Length: 53 in. (134.5 cm.)
Purchase 138:1947

Montorsoli's *Reclining Pan* is one of the
finest examples of Italian Renaissance
sculpture in the United States. A student
of Michelangelo, Montorsoli executed a
number of fountains based on mythological themes, among them the *Pan,* which
was intended for a rustic garden or grotto.
As the woodland god of pastures and
flocks, Pan is represented as a satyr, a
man-goat hybrid. He holds his attribute,
the "pan-pipes," a wind instrument of
cut reeds bound together. He also is
identified by the faun skin draped over

his shoulders; the animal's head is visible
near Pan's left hand.

The sculpture reveals the influence of
Michelangelo, particularly in the satyr's
grimacing face, pronounced musculature,
and powerful left hand. Montorsoli has
enlivened the figure by using colored
marbles to accent Pan's horns, his hooves,
and the faun's hooves knotted across his
chest. The artist was able to give this
piece a distinctly antique flavor. In fact,
his ability to mimic antiquity was affirmed
in the seventeenth century when the
Reclining Pan was mistakenly identified
as an example of second-century Hellenistic sculpture, a label that continued to
this century. Interestingly, Montorsoli
carved his masterpiece from a piece of
antique statuary, and traces of drapery
and a fringe are still visible on the back.

Giorgio Vasari, Italian, 1511–1574
Judith and Holofernes, c.1554
Oil on panel
42½ x 31½ in. (108 x 80 cm.)
Purchase: Friends Fund and Funds given
in honor of Betty Greenfield Grossman
2:1982

Perhaps best known as the biographer of Italian Renaissance artists, Giorgio Vasari was also a leading Florentine intellectual, painter, and architect. He received important commissions for mural cycles in Florence and Rome, but some of his best work is found in more modestly scaled panel paintings. One such work is his *Judith and Holofernes,* dated to 1554 in the artist's account book.

The Old Testament story of the beautiful Judith, who tricked and then slew the tyrant Holofernes, was a popular subject for sixteenth-century artists. Vasari's version depicts the moment before Judith strikes the sleeping general. Her handmaid assists by pulling the curtain from behind. As was typical of the Mannerist style, Vasari grouped the figures closely together, compressing them into a confined space. The painting is a demonstration of the artist's compositional skill and his ability to portray the muscular human body, evident both in the build of Holofernes and in Judith's back and arms. The figure of Judith, incidentally, can be traced to Michelangelo's Sistine ceiling. Vasari, a student of Michelangelo, often had occasion to draw upon the lessons of the master in composing his works.

Orazio Gentileschi, Italian, 1565–1647
Danaë, c.1611–1612
Oil on copper
16 x 20⁷⁄₁₆ in. (40.5 x 52.5 cm.)
Purchase: Museum Funds, by exchange;
Gift of Edward Mallinckrodt, Sydney
M. Shoenberg, Horace Morison, Mrs.
Florence E. Bing, Morton D. May in
honor of Perry T. Rathbone, James Lee
Johnson, Oscar Johnson, Fredonia J.
Moss, Mrs. Arthur Drefs, Mrs. W. Welles
Hoyt, Mr. J. Lionberger Davis, Jacob M.
Heimann, Virginia Linn Bullock in
memory of her husband, George Benbow
Bullock, C. Wickham Moore, Mrs. Lyda
D'Oench Turley and Miss Elizabeth
F. D'Oench, and J. Harold Pettus, by
exchange; and bequests of Mrs. Alfred
Keller and Cora E. Ludwig, by exchange
93:1986

According to an ancient Greek myth,
King Arcisius of Argos was warned by an
oracle that his beautiful daughter Danaë
would bear a son who would kill him. To
prevent her from ever having a child, the
fearful king locked his daughter into a
dark underground chamber. One night,
however, the god Zeus surreptitiously
visited Danaë by transforming himself
into a golden shower to gain entrance to
her bed. The result of this divine union
was Perseus, who later fulfilled the
oracle's prophecy by accidentally killing
his grandfather with a discus. Danaë is
showered not with rain but with gold
coins that her attendant greedily collects.

This painting is either the work of
Orazio Gentileschi, one of the most
influential followers of Caravaggio, or the
work of Gentileschi's talented daughter
Artemisia. Father and daughter shared a
style marked by steadfast naturalism and
powerful use of light and shadow. The
subtle manipulation of tones and masterful handling of the flesh and fabric effect
a beautiful luminosity, specifically characteristic of Orazio's art. Danaë's erotic
pose and fierce clutching of the gold
coins, however, make her the most overtly sensual and aggressive representation
of this mythological heroine. This detail
suggests the hand of Artemisia, who
often reinterpreted traditional female
types.

The Bird Catcher, c.1600
Italian, after Giovanni da Bologna,
Flemish, 1529–1608
Gilt bronze
Height: 12¹/₁₆ in. (30.6 cm.)
Purchase 284:1951

One of the major figures of late sixteenth-century sculpture in Italy was
not an Italian but a Flemish artist, Jean
Boulogne, better known by his Italian
nickname, Giambologna. His work in
stone and in bronze is characterized by
daring composition, sensual surfaces, and
technical virtuosity. *The Bird Catcher* is
of such exceptional quality that it may
reflect the actual hand of Giambologna;
at the least, it is based on a design by the
master. The bronze is among the best of
approximately ten examples known; it is
set apart by the subtlety of surface, sensitive modeling in the face and neck, and
carefully planned contours in the tunic
and breeches.

The figure, who wears simple country
clothes and has been outfitted with a
variety of birdcatching devices, is more of
a generic "bird catcher" than a hunter in
pursuit of prey. The stick in his right
hand is most likely intended for forcing
the birds from their nests. The catcher's
other attributes include a leather pouch
attached to his waist, a dead bird hung
on his belt, and a cage held aloft in his
left hand.

Typical of Giambologna are the
compositional rhythms achieved by the
advancing left arm and right leg in coun-
terbalance with the receding right arm
and left leg. Fabric folds create engaging
diagonals that encourage the viewer to
observe the figure from multiple points
of view. The meticulous surface treatment and fine workmanship make this
piece a good example of the highly prized
objects that motivated collectors in the
sixteenth and seventeenth centuries.

Antonio Canal, called Canaletto, Italian,
1697–1768
**Capriccio: An Island in the Lagoon
with a Pavilion and a Church**
Oil on canvas
20 x 27 in. (51 x 68.5 cm.)
Purchase: Friends Fund 12:1967

Antonio Canal, known as Canaletto,
specialized in views of Venice and the
Venetian countryside. The English in
particular coveted images of the views
and ruins they had admired on their
visits to Italy. Sometimes, these scenes
were inspired by but not faithful to the
topographical details they purported to
document. They were imaginary combinations of landscape and landmarks,
known by the Italian term *capricci*. The
seemingly precise line of Canaletto's
architecture often denies these scenes a
sense of fanciful invention; they mas-
querade as recorded fact.

In the St. Louis painting, the artist
has combined the Venetian lagoon with
some buildings from nearby Padua and
a campanile from yet another source to
produce a grouping of simple structure
and subtle balance. The light, as always
in Canaletto's work, is an important
element of the painting. It bathes the
buildings in radiant tones and confers
upon the whole an almost unnaturalistic
clarity. Human figures are secondary
players in this carefully contrived arrangement. Their casual poses as they
pursue various tasks belie their careful
placement in the structural logic of the
whole; at times they even echo the larger
architectural forms. The virtuoso handling of paint, the warmth and clarity of
the light, and the mastery of composition
make Canaletto's paintings as appealing
today as they were to his eighteenth-
century clients.

Francisco de Zurbarán, Spanish,
1598–1664
St. Francis Standing with a Skull,
after 1634
Oil on canvas
36 x 12 in. (91.5 x 30.5 cm.)
Purchase 47:1941

The Museum's *St. Francis Standing with a
Skull* is one of four paintings known to
have been executed by Zurbarán for the
altar of the Carmelite church of the
College of San Alberto in Seville, Spain.
Saint Teresa of Avila, the great sixteenth-
century Spanish mystic and founder of
the Carmelite order, based her reforms
on Franciscan spirituality. Central to St.
Teresa's method was intense contemplation aimed at progressively approaching
union with the divine. The Catholic
Church's Council of Trent, which ended
in 1563, urged that St. Francis be represented simply, as a model to encourage
the contemplative life. Zurbarán's intense
single figure of the saint, removed from
any reference to time or place, captures
the spirit of such religious devotion.

The St. Louis version is the first of
several images of St. Francis that Zurbarán
painted. It is marked by strong contrasts
of light and dark, with an elevated light
source bathing the hood, sleeves, and
shoulders of the saint's brown robe. He
is aligned perfectly with the center of the
painting, an axis reinforced by his down-
turned gaze as he contemplates the skull
in his hands. Zurbarán removes St.
Francis from the space of the viewer
by allowing his bowed head to keep his
eyes in shadow. He is a model for piety,
not a vehicle for prayer, and the viewer
remains outside the saint's realm, unable
to penetrate the rigorous and single-
minded contemplative act.

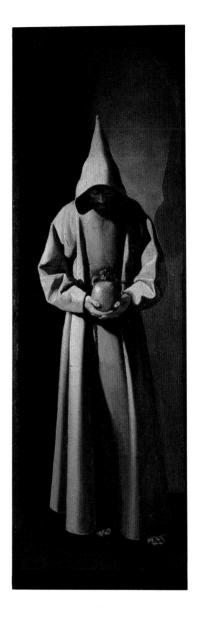

■

Jacob Cornelisz. van Oostsanen, Dutch,
active c.1500–1533
Saint Mary Magdalene, 1519
Oil on panel
19⅛ x 15¾ in. (48.6 x 40 cm.)
Inscribed on column, upper left:
Anno Dni 1519
Gift of Edward Mallinckrodt 138:1922

Jacob Cornelisz. van Oostsanen, famous
for his paintings and woodcuts, was
Amsterdam's first renowned artistic personality. His style, well represented in
Saint Mary Magdalene, was based on
meticulously rendered surfaces, evocative
textures, and precise detail. These characteristics are evident in the Magdalene's
richly embroidered bodice and headdress,
as well as in her jewelry and the tapestry
that covers the foreground ledge.

The painting, signed and dated 1519,
is one of the earliest known single representations of St. Mary Magdalene, who
was a favored subject for devotional
prayer in the sixteenth and seventeenth
centuries. The Magdalene, a faithful
follower of Christ after having been a
prostitute, was considered a worthy example of someone who had erred and
then had been saved by turning to Christ.
She was a particularly appropriate model
during the Reformation, since she per-
sonified the hope of salvation even for
those who might have strayed from the
faith. She is usually portrayed with an
ointment jar, an allusion to her sensual
pursuits. The artist has added other clues
to her past in the carved panel beneath
the arched opening, which shows nudes
carousing. This reference to Mary Magdalene's sin is balanced by the figure seen
through the arch, a depiction of the saint
in her later life as a hermit who has
rejected physical pleasures.

Hans Holbein the Younger, German,
1497/98–1543
Mary, Lady Guildeford, 1527
Oil on panel
34¼ x 27¾ in. (87 x 70.6 cm.)
Purchase 1:1943

Hans Holbein the Younger left a remarkable visual record of the court of Henry
VIII of England in scores of drawings
and, more rarely, paintings. This likeness
of Mary Wotten, wife of the powerful
Comptroller of the Royal Household, Sir
Henry Guildeford, is among the finest of
Holbein's portraits. Painted in 1527 during the artist's first visit to England, it is
contemporary with his famous portraits
of his host and patron, Sir Thomas More.

Lady Guildeford's portrait exhibits
those qualities that were to make Holbein
the favorite of the Tudor court. He drew
on his Northern heritage for the meticulous description of surface textures, capturing in paint the feel of velvet, linen,
metal, pearls, and jewels, all of which
bespeak the sitter's wealth and social
standing. The use of costly gold pigment
in the sleeves, the chains draped around
the bodice, the necklaces and rings, and
the pearl-trimmed headpiece convey
an even greater sense of luxury.

Holbein's sure sense of monumental
form, derived from his study of Italian
Renaissance art, imposes order and clarity on the abundance of surface detail.
Underlying the composition is a stable
pyramid defined by the black veil, the
overdress, and the hands held before the
body. Holbein shows that he was one of
the first Northern artists to appreciate
Italian painting as more than merely a
source for fashionable details, like the
classical columns in the background.

Jan van Goyen, Dutch, 1596–1656
On the Ice Near Dordrecht, 1643
Oil on oak panel
14¾ x 13½ in. (36.5 x 33.4 cm.)
Purchase 223:1916

Jan van Goyen depicted the city of
Dordrecht more frequently than any
other recognizable town scene. This view
of Dordrecht is somewhat unusual, in
that it is from the north rather than the
south. The true subject of this painting,
however, is the subtle variation of tones
found in the cloudy sky. During the early
1640s, van Goyen depicted winter landscapes often, with a palette that was limited in color but greatly varied in tonal
range. The grayish-brown atmosphere
achieved in this painting is characteristic
of the artist. The choice of a vertical
rather than horizontal format is unusual
for his work of this period, however.

Although it is small – a cabinet picture, as such are often called – *On the Ice
Near Dordrecht* is one of van Goyen's best
efforts. The sky billows upward, and the
viewer is at once caught up in the vast
space above the flat land; the subtlety of
color and the delicacy of feeling draw the
eye into the scene. While the scale of the
figures is somewhat larger than in van
Goyen's other views of Dordrecht, man is
still a small part of this paean to nature,
rendered in a soft, monochromatic color
scheme so like the Dutch winter.

Balthasar van der Ast, Dutch,
c.1590–1657
Floral Still Life with Shells, 1622
Oil on copper
13⅛ x 8¾ in. (33.5 x 22.2 cm.)
Purchase 172:1955

A specialist in still-life painting, Balthasar
van der Ast learned his craft from his
brother-in-law, Ambrosius Bosschaert the
Elder (1573–1621). In this tiny painting,
done the year following Bosschaert's
death, van der Ast remained faithful to
the style of his late master; the flat, delicate patterns of linear arabesques and the
hard, brilliant colors are a legacy of the
older artist. Van der Ast eventually abandoned this conservative manner in favor
of more convincing three-dimensional
still lifes, but he rarely surpassed the
naive charm and freshness of this early
work.

Although each blossom is depicted
with scientific exactitude, the bouquet
was not painted from direct observation.
The showy striped tulips, for example,
which were fabulously expensive at the
time, were most likely not raised by the
artist. He probably would have gone to a
grower to make sketches. Because the
flowers shown bloom at different times of
the year, individual studies would have
been executed for each.

The almost obsessive verisimilitude of
the flowers is equalled by the painstaking
details of the moth and fly, the glass
container, and even the worm-eaten
wood of the table. Colorful shells like
those in the lower right, native to Asia
and America, evoke the global commer-
cial empire that supported Dutch prosperity in the seventeenth century. For all
his fidelity to visual facts, however, van
der Ast achieves in this painting a quiet
poetry that transcends mere illustration.

■

François Boucher, French, 1703–1770
The Dovecote, 1758
Oil on canvas
17⅞ x 27³/₁₆ in. (45.4 x 69.1 cm.)
Purchase 75:1937

Few artists were ever so completely in sympathy with the tastes and values of their patrons as François Boucher. A delightful landscape painted at the height of Boucher's career, this painting is just the sort of confection that made him the favorite of Louis XIV's mistress Madame de Pompadour and her fashionable circle. The dovecote tower and other elements of the composition are based perhaps on sketches made from life, but this is no record of a particular place. Instead, Boucher has conjured up an enchanted garden, as charming as it is unreal. The idealized conception of country life expressed in this painting was shared by Boucher's patrons, who, to amuse themselves, would sometimes don rustic costumes and play at milking cows or tending sheep.

Color is a key ingredient in creating the painting's delectable illusion, from the deep blue-green foliage against the frosted blue sky to the touches of pale pink and bright coral. Boucher's masterful manipulation of light and shadow and the undulating curves that animate the sky, the trees, and even the rickety bridge bespeak the plausibility of this impossible world, so fluently rendered in short strokes of thickly applied paint.

Enthusiasm for charming yet highly artificial works like this one was not universal among Boucher's contemporaries. To the philosophers of the Enlightenment, such bonbons were symptomatic of the moral and intellectual flabbiness of the French ruling class.

Jean-Honoré Fragonard, French,
1732–1806
The Washerwomen (The Laundresses),
1756–1761
Oil on canvas
24¼ x 28¾ in. (61.5 x 73 cm.)
Purchase 76:1937

Whether celebrating the refined pastimes
of the French upper classes or depicting a
scene from a distinctly lower stratum of
society, Jean-Honoré Fragonard painted
with great panache and vigor. It is only a
slight misrepresentation of the artist's
intentions to state that paint itself is the
true subject of Fragonard's works. The
reality of the hot, backbreaking monotony
of boiling and washing clothes has been
banished from this charming picture;
what impresses the viewer is the exuberant flurry of brushstrokes. Just over a
century later, Edgar Degas treated the
same subject, but he wanted to commu-
nicate the human toll of such grinding
labor. The change in emphasis illustrates
the vast difference between the sensibili-

ties of the pre-Revolutionary era and the
modern world.

This painting dates from the early
years of Fragonard's career, when he was
living in Italy. What appears to be an
offhand sketch, dashed off at the scene,
is in fact very carefully and deliberately
composed: the main figures form a stable
triangle, circumscribed by the arc of the
vaulted ceiling. This underlying geometric structure reflects Fragonard's as-
similation of the traditions of the Italian
Renaissance. The apparent spontaneity
of the picture comes from the artist's use
of deftly applied dabs and squiggles of
paint to define forms. With a flick of his
loaded brush, Fragonard could suggest
the sheen of the dog's sleek coat, the
differing quality of sunshine and firelight,
or the vaporous atmosphere of the laun-
dry. Faces, hands, even entire bodies were
created with a single stroke. It was this
virtuosity that aroused the admiration of
his contemporaries and still enchants
today.

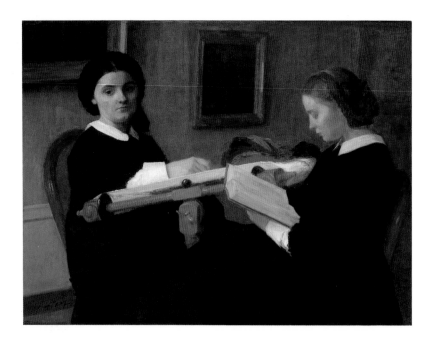

Henri Fantin-Latour, French, 1836–1904
The Two Sisters, 1859
Oil on canvas
38⁹/₁₆ x 51³/₁₆ in. (98 x 130 cm.)
Purchase 8:1937

Although best known for flower paintings, Henri Fantin-Latour established his
reputation through portraits. The St.
Louis portrait depicts the artist's two
sisters, Natalie, shown embroidering,
and Marie, shown reading. It is one of
Fantin-Latour's earliest scenes of family
life, and was finished just before an attack of mental illness sent Natalie to an
asylum for the remainder of her life.

The appeal of Fantin-Latour's still-life
flower paintings derives from his sureness
of touch and the tender fragility of the
blossoms. Such a sensibility is evident in
this portrait, where Natalie gazes out of
the picture space, a suggestion of malaise
slightly clouding her face. The eye of a
still-life artist can also be detected in the
careful arrangement of the two girls. One
sits in profile while the other turns to
face the viewer, making the figures vertical accents that bracket the horizontal
embroidery frame. The composition is
dominated by rhythms of light and dark
in the bodices and collars as well as the
faces and hair.

■

Thomas Gainsborough, English,
1727–1788
View in Suffolk, c.1755
Oil on canvas
37 x 49½ in. (94 x 125.8 cm.)
The John Fowler Memorial Collection,
Bequest of Cora Liggett Fowler 168:1928

Landscape painting had only recently
been established as an independent art
form in Britain when Thomas Gainsborough created this luminous view of the
Suffolk countryside in the 1750s. It was
still difficult for an English artist to sell
enough landscapes to make a decent
living, so Gainsborough, like most
English painters, supported himself by
doing portraits. Though landscape painting would remain for him an unprofit-
able sideline, Gainsborough was by far
the most original and inventive English
landscapist of the eighteenth century.

When he executed this early work,
the artist was under the spell of contemporary French painting, which he would
have seen in London collections. The
influence of François Boucher especially
is apparent in the sinuous curves that
twist and ripple through the composition, animating every element. Also tied
to French sensibilities is the treatment
of the countryside as an elegant park,
populated by carefree peasants like the
handsome pair courting in the foreground. This modish artificiality, however,
is tempered by Gainsborough's familiari-
ty with the more naturalistic Dutch
landscape tradition and, more impor-
tantly, by his own direct observations.
Only the example of nature could have
provided a model for the convincing
sensation of warm light filtered through
a dense atmosphere, and of summer heat
and moisture-laden clouds, impressions
strengthened by the predominance of
rich orange and brown tones. Gainsborough's empathy with nature transcends
conventional, imported formulas and
looks ahead to the great achievements of
English landscape painters of the nineteenth century.

■

John Martin, English, 1789–1854
**Sadak in Search of the Waters of
Oblivion,** 1812
Oil on canvas
72 x 49½ in. (182.9 x 125.7 cm.)
Purchase: Friends Fund 1566:1983

Executed in London for the 1812 Royal
Academy Exhibition, this painting was
the first ambitious canvas for which
Martin achieved recognition. In keeping
with the early nineteenth-century English
taste for Oriental exoticism and the grandeur of untamed nature, Martin conceived a vast, imaginative landscape
where man is overwhelmed by the scale
and power of natural forces.

The fictional subject is taken from
the popular *Tales of the Genii* (1762), in
which the noble Persian Sadak labors to
free his wife from a wicked Sultan. Sadak
seeks the waters of Oblivion, whose mag-
ical powers can vanquish his evil foe.
Martin has depicted Sadak struggling
toward the remote heights of his goal.
The majesty of the rocky facets, the
powerful coloring, and the lurid white
highlights depict a world that is both
dangerous and beautiful, reflecting both
the Romantic reverence for nature and
fear of its awesome power.

■

Sir Edwin Henry Landseer, R.A., British,
1802–1873
Attachment, 1829
Oil on canvas
39 x 31¼ in. (99 x 79.5 cm.)
Purchase: Gift of Mrs. Eugene A. Perry
in memory of her mother, Mrs. Claude
Kirkpatrick, by exchange 123:1987

Sir Edwin Landseer, considered in his
day England's greatest painter, was
known for his engaging animal images
and portraits of pets, including those of
Queen Victoria. Dogs are particularly
prominent in his work, and none of his
canine heroes so well captures the spirit
of Victorian sentiment as the terrier
depicted in *Attachment.* The painting is
an illustration of Sir Walter Scott's short
poem "Helvellyn," the story of a young
man's tragic death in 1805 and his faithful

terrier's long vigil beside the lifeless body.
The young man suffered an accidental
fall while on a climbing expedition to the
Helvellyn mountain in Scotland's Lake
District, and his remains lay undiscov-
ered for three months. Scott's poem is
the only account of the incident; no
additional verification has ever appeared.

As depicted by Landseer, the story's
setting is a dramatic backdrop of stormy
sky and large imposing faces of bare rock
that suggest dizzying heights. The body
lies close to the edge of a high cliff, and
the juxtaposition of strong light and
looming shadow heightens the drama.
The brightly colored areas direct the
viewer's gaze to the attentive canine, who
gingerly paws at her master's windswept
cloak in hopes of some response.

Decorative Arts

■

Cassone, 15th century
Italian
English walnut, white oak, euonymus,
fruit woods, parchment
Height: 36 in. (91.4 cm.)
Purchase 21:1930

The term *cassone* refers to all sizes of
both ornamented and undecorated
hinged-top chests used to store household articles like clothing, linen, books,
and tools. These were the most common
pieces of domestic furniture during the
Italian Renaissance, and other than beds,
often the most prominent objects in a
room. Large, elaborate *cassoni* frequently
comprised the major part of a dowry.
Decoration took the form of vigorous
carving, painted scenes, or inlaid woods

and gilt-gesso ornament. Most compositions were borrowed from ancient and
Roman history.

In shape, this *cassone* resembles a
Roman sarcophagus. The oak-leaf wreath
inlaid at the center of the lid derives
from Roman monuments and indicates
the chest was part of a dowry. The arms
depicted on the corner pilasters are probably those of Sigismondo Malatesta
(1417–1468). Strongly architectural in
appearance, *cassoni* of this size reflect the
scale and design of the halls in which
they stood.

Pair of Stirrups, 1555
Austrian, Augsburg
Gilt bronze
Each height: 6½ in. (16.4 cm.)
Purchase 54,55:1926

This pair of stirrups was part of a complete parade armor garniture, one of four made for Emperor Ferdinand I of Austria (1503–1564) and his three sons. This pair probably belonged to the emperor's youngest son, Archduke Charles II. All eight stirrups, cast in the same mold, were crafted of pure bronze and decorated in low and high relief with heavy gilding. The elaborate ornament of female and animal figures amongst fruit and scrolls is based on a standard decorative style developed in Italy before 1500, derived from Roman prototypes.

Pierre Reymond, French, Limoges, 1513–1599
Tazza with Cover: c. 1560
Enamel on copper, ormolu, gilt
Diameter: 7¼ in. (18.4 cm.)
Purchase: Gift of Mr. and Mrs. Stanley Lopata 221:1986

Production of painted enamels flourished in Limoges, France, from approximately 1450 through the seventeenth century. Biblical stories were common subjects for the decoration of enamels. This tazza illustrates two Old Testament scenes: inside the dish, Jethro observes his son-in-law Moses listening to the Israelites' problems (Exodus 18), while on the lid, Absalom flees the servants of his father, David (II Samuel 18).

In the process of crafting enamel pieces, colors were applied separately and allowed to dry on the metal object that served as a base. The enamel was fused onto the surface by firing; since dark colors required longer firing times than light ones, a number of successive firings was performed on each piece.

Drinking Glass, 1580–1600
Italian, Venice
Glass
Height: 9 in. (22.9 cm.)
Purchase: Museum Purchase, by
exchange 43:1989

Before the sixteenth century, glass ornamentation usually was limited to engraving, enameling, gilding, or decoration
applied to the surface of a finished object. A significant development by early
sixteenth-century Venetian glassmakers
was a translucent milky-white glass used
for decoration; the glassmakers themselves embedded canes of the opaque
white glass *(lattimo)* within clear glass.
This extremely delicate technique remained popular well into the seventeenth
century and was imitated by artisans in
Germany and the Netherlands, where the
method was known as *façon de Venise.*

Peter Öhr I, German
Tankard, 1640–1660
Silver, silver gilt
Height: 9⅞ in. (25.1 cm.)
Purchase: Funds given by the Decorative
Arts Society; Mrs. John S. Lehmann,
Mr. and Mrs. Robert B. Smith, Dr. Alvin
R. Brown, and other donors to the 1988
Annual Appeal 37:1989

Massive silver gilt tankards with high-
relief decoration were characteristic of
northern Germany during the second
half of the seventeenth century. The
ornamentation on this tankard, intended
for display rather than use, relates closely
to that of contemporary carved ivory
tankards fitted with silver mounts. The
vigorous repoussé decoration, in which
the metal is displaced outwards by ham-
mering from the inside, stretches the
silver and the skill of the craftsman nearly to their limits. To protect the thin
outer wall, such tankards have a smooth-
sided interior wall.

Half-Suit of Armor, early 17th century
Italian
Steel
Height: 27 in. (68.5 cm.)
Purchase 230:1923

By the fifteenth century, jousting tournaments had developed from training exercises into an organized sport, a showcase for personal bravery and skill. Tournaments included duels between individual contestants as well as combat between groups of knights, either on horseback or on foot.

This half-suit of armor was originally part of a harness used for foot tournaments at the "barriers." The contestants, armed with polearms or swords, would be separated by a bar set at waist height, the "barriers." Strikes below the waist were forbidden, which eliminated the need for defenses on the lower half of the body.

Pieces surviving from this suit are the close helmet, collar, breastplate, backplate, and right and left arm defenses. Half-moons, the emblem of the Strozzi family of Florence, are painted over the entire surface, a decorative technique rare on armor. Three wax inventory seals of the Strozzi armory can still be seen inside.

David Bessmann, German,
active 1640–1677
Nautilus Beaker, 1645–1650
Silver, gilt
Height: 14 in. (35.6 cm.)
Purchase: Gift of Misses Effie and Stella
Kuhn 79:1954

Although examples of nautilus cups are
known from the Middle Ages, most of
these lavish and opulent objects were
produced in the sixteenth and seventeenth centuries. Typically, these cups
incorporated actual nautilus shells into
elaborately decorated frames of silver or
gold, sometimes encrusted with jewels
or embellished with enamel. Nautilus
shells had been imported to Europe for
several centuries, but increased trade
with the Far East in the sixteenth century
made them more available.

This cup is of a rarer type in which
the shell itself is fashioned of silver, an
appealing conceit in an age that revered
the artificial reproduction of natural
forms. Decorative motifs for these cups
generally included sea creatures such as
dolphins, sea horses, and sea serpents,
although satyrs and eagles also were popular adornments. Our cup includes a
triton rising out of the water to support
the shell on his head and steady it with
his left hand. The piece is gilded except
for the triton's upper torso, a technique
known as parcel (partial) gilding.

Nautilus cups had a twofold purpose:
to demonstrate the wealth and taste of
the patron and to display the technical
skill of the artist. While the patron of
this piece has not been identified, the
pinecone stamp visible on the shell rim
indicates that the cup was fashioned in
Augsburg between 1645 and 1650. During
the seventeenth century, Nürnberg and
Augsburg were the two major German
centers for decorative and silver work.
The cup also bears the mark of the silversmith, David Bessmann, who worked in
Augsburg between 1640 and 1677.

King Ahasuerus and Queen Esther,
c.1660
English
Silk, metallic threads, glass
13⅝ x 10¼ in. (26 x 35 cm.)
Gift of Mrs. William A. McDonnell
17:1968

Stumpwork, an embroidery technique popular in Europe between 1650 and 1690, is distinctive for its three-dimensional effects, provided by raised metal-thread embroidery, areas of buttonhole stitch only partly attached to the ground, padding, metal strips, and wooden or ivory faces and hands for figures. Glass beads and pearls add opulence to these embroideries, which usually were crafted by young girls.

Biblical subjects and stories from Ovid provided the favorite themes for stumpwork, and published engravings served as a major design source. The scene depicted in this embroidery is typical, with each figure perched on its own patch of grass amidst disproportionately large flowers, insects, and animals. Queen Esther, dressed as a noble lady from the court of Charles II, is interceding with her husband King Ahasuerus on behalf of her fellow Jews whom he had condemned to death, including her relative Mordecai, who stands behind the throne.

■

Sitting Room, 1731
French, Paris
Oak paneling
262 x 175 in. (665.5 x 444.5 cm.)
Purchase 7:1929

Jean Galliard de la Bouexière, a country squire of minor nobility, went to Paris in 1731 to seek his fortune and a position in the court of Louis XIV. He purchased a town house and property in a fashionable section of the city, at the corner of rue d'Antin and rue Casanova. Over the next six years he enlarged and updated the house, adding *boiseries* (carved woodwork) in several rooms, including this second floor *cabinet*. *Cabinets* functioned as studies, dressing rooms, or personal sitting rooms. This sitting room was adjacent to de la Bouexière's bedroom.

Boiseries in formal rooms were painted white with moldings highlighted in gold, but this *cabinet* and the adjoining bedroom were decorated more simply. The moldings are delicately carved in the lively curves and arabesques of the Rococo style. The mirror frames may have been designed by Robert de Cotte (1656–1735), architect to Louis XV.

De la Bouexière collected paintings by well-known artists of the time. The three canvases placed above two of the mirrors and the doors of this room are attributed to Charles Antoine Coypel (1694–1752), an eighteenth-century French painter known for his elaborate interior decorative schemes.

Pedestal Clock, 1720–1735
French
Case in the manner of André-Charles
Boulle, French, 1642–1732; works by Jean
Godde, French, 1668–1748
Ebony, gilt bronze, brass, tortoise-shell,
glass
Height: 99¼ in. (252.1 cm.)
Purchase: Friends Fund 32: 1989 a–g

André-Charles Boulle worked as a cabinet-maker to Louis XIV from 1672 to
1725. The royal appontment released
Boulle from guild restrictions that ordi-
narily limited a workshop to a single type
of production. Boulle was allowed to
design cabinetry as well as bronze
mounts, resulting in highly integrated
works.

Boulle is most famous for a marquetry, originally developed in Italy, in
which the carcass of the furniture is
veneered in tortoise-shell and metal,
usually brass, cut in intricate, often figural shapes. The tortoise-shell and metal
are laid together and sawed simultaneously, resulting in the same designs in
both materials. Boulle's expertise in this
technique made him the first cabinet-
maker to give his name to a furniture
style. Production of marquetry in the
manner of Boulle continued until the
late nineteenth century.

Boulle supplied many pieces of furniture for the royal apartments at Versailles,
and also accepted private commissions
from French noblemen and wealthy
patrons. Several motifs in the marquetry
and the mounts of the clock suggest an
association with Louis XIV: Apollo's
head within a sunburst was the self-
appropriated symbol of the French king;
the crane, an attribute of monarchs,
represented vigilance; and the fleur-de-lis
was a characteristic emblem of the
French royal family.

Lappets with Frill, 1750–1760
Flemish, Brussels
Linen, bobbin lace
88 x 3½ in. (223.5 x 8.9 cm.)
Gift of Paul Ullman and Marian
Cronheim 77:1976.105

During the eighteenth century, lace denoted wealth and taste in both men's and
women's apparel. A fashionable female
headdress of the period consisted of a
cap back, a gathered frill surrounding
the face, and lappets which draped down
the sides or back of the head. Few complete sets exist today, and even lappets
with the linking frill are rare.

Flemish lace dominated the market
due to the superiority of Flemish thread,
the fortunate result of geography and
climate. Brussels bobbin lace developed a
distinctive mesh ground of a slightly
elongated, hexagonal shape. Also characteristic of Brussels bobbin lace are the
raised edges to the designs.

Covered Vase, 1768–1770
French, Sèvres
Porcelain and ormolu (gilt bronze)
Height: 17¼ in. (43.9 cm.)
Purchase: Gift of Mrs. Sarah Jane May
Waldheim, by exchange 98:1985

In 1756, the Manufacture Royale de
Porcelaine moved from the Château de
Vincennes to Sèvres; three years later the
financially troubled factory became the
personal property of King Louis XV.

The rich ground colors used at Sèvres
are especially distinctive. This vase is
decorated in dark blue *(bleu du roi)* with
a chain of light-blue *(bleu celeste)* ovals
around the center. Of the French porcelain factories, only the Manufacture
Royale was legally entitled to use gold
in its decoration. The finely tooled gilding on the St. Louis vase testifies to the
extraordinary skill of the craftsmen
employed at Sèvres.

Jean-Henri Riesener, German, 1734–1806
Corner Cabinet *(Encoignure),* 1780–1785
Oak, mahogany veneer, gilt bronze,
marble
Height: 35¹³/₁₆ in. (91 cm.)
Purchase 117:1945

In 1768, Jean-Henri Riesener achieved in
France the status of master *ébéniste,* or
cabinet-maker, specializing in veneered
furniture. He was one of the greatest
ébénistes of his time, and worked extensively for Louis XVI between 1775 and
1785. This *encoignure,* or corner cabinet,
was one of a set of four made for the
salon on the second floor of Queen
Marie-Antoinette's house in the Hamlet
on the grounds of the Petit Trianon at
Versailles. The Hamlet, a miniature village designed by Richard Mique, was the
most informal and picturesque of the
Queen's retreats from court life. All four

cabinets survive – one at The Art Institute of Chicago and two signed ones in
the collection of the Grand Duke of
Mecklenburg – and are the only known
original furnishings of the Hamlet.

Corner cabinets were typically made
in pairs, and often *en suite* with com-
modes, large chests of drawers. The furnishings in the buildings of the Hamlet
were simpler and more modest than
those of other royal residences. In the
case of this cabinet, simple mahogany
veneer replaces elaborately patterned
marquetry, and the gilt-bronze mounts
are fewer and more restrained. They are
attributed to Pierre-Philippe Thomire
(1751–1843) or Pierre Gouthière (1732–
1812/14), premier metal casters known to
have supplied mounts for royal furniture.

■

Wedgwood, English, 1759–present
Vase, 1785–1795
Stoneware: jasper
Height: 7¾ in. (19.7 cm.)
Gift of Mr. and Mrs. Milton L. Zorensky
266:1989

In 1759, Josiah Wedgwood founded
the firm which still bears his name. Perhaps his most famous achievement was
the development in 1775 of a dense white
stoneware known as jasperware, which
could be fired at a slightly higher temper-
ature than other stonewares, becoming
translucent like porcelain.

Neoclassical and Romantic artists
were inspired by contemporary excavations at Pompeii and Herculaneum, and
ruins became a common architectural
form. The fashion also pervaded the decorative arts, as exemplified by this vase.
Such pieces were made in single and
triple versions as well as the double type
illustrated here. Although they functioned ornamentally as contrived ruins,
they also served as flower-holders.

■

Anthony R. Rasch, American, born
Bavaria, 1778–1859
Tea Caddy, c.1807
Silver
Height: 7 in. (18 cm.)
Purchase: Funds given by the Decorative
Arts Society, Mr. and Mrs. George
S. Rosborough, Jr., and Mrs. Mason
Scudder 66:1969

Following the American War of Indepen-
dence, the new nation sought inspiration
from classical Rome to bring to its political and cultural life an emphasis on order
and balance. The design of this tea caddy
derives from a classical sarcophagus.
Neoclassical motifs decorate it: rams'
heads and hooves, guilloche swags, an-
themions, and a leaf medallion. Rasch
used a sheet of rolled silver for the sides
of this caddy; the lid, bottom, and base
were raised in the traditional manner.

Flagon, 1844
Designed by William Butterfield,
English, 1814–1900
Fashioned by John James Keith, English,
active 1824–1880s
Silver gilt
Height: 10⅜ in. (26.4 cm.)
Purchase: Donors to the 1985 Annual
Appeal 153:1989

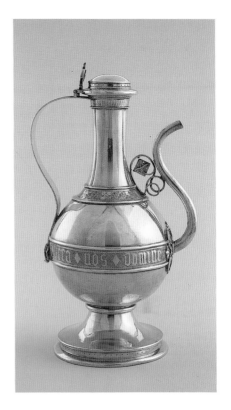

In 1818, the British Parliament passed the
Million Pound Act to provide funds for
the construction and improvement of
churches in highly populated and urban
areas, with the intention of reversing a
sharp decrease in church attendance and
reestablishing religion as a positive force
for social control. Over 10,000 church
building programs were undertaken
between the 1820s and 1860s by architects such as A.W.N. Pugin and William
Butterfield, resulting in an unparalleled
revival of religious architecture and decorative arts.

   In 1843, William Butterfield was
charged by the Cambridge Camden
Society to develop a plan to improve
architecture and furnishings for the
Anglican Church. His designs reflect the
influence of Gothic and medieval sources
and demonstrate the importance placed
by the Society on liturgical accoutre-
ments.

   This flagon, similar to a piece published in Butterfield's *Instrumenta Ecclesi-
astica* of 1847, shows Victorian church
plate design at its most striking, with
articulated surfaces, engraved decoration,
and curvaceous forms. The flagon, executed by silversmith John James Keith,
is inscribed around the base: "Bisham
Parish Church, Diocese of Oxford, a
thanksgiving for recovery from sickness."
It also bears the Latin inscription "libera
nos domine ab omni peccato" (Deliver us
Lord from sin).

Dining Room, c.1795, remodeled 1808
American, Salem
Wallpaper, French, 1815
Pine
201 x 176 in. (510.5 x 447 cm.)
Purchase 19:1931

This room came from a three-story
tavern building still standing at 94 Boston Street in Salem, Massachusetts. It
was a private dining room situated on
the second floor.

Daniel Frye, the tavern's owner, was
an entrepreneur and miller as well as an
innkeeper. In 1790 Frye purchased the
Boston Street site and five years later replaced the existing building with a new
structure. Around 1808 he hired Samuel
McIntire, the preeminent furniture maker and carver in Salem, to install new
woodwork and mantels in this and another room of the inn. The carved and
painted fruit basket on the mantel is a
typical McIntire motif, as are the reproduced wheat sheaves.

Frye died in 1813; in 1817 the house
was sold to Jacob Putnam, wealthy mer-

chant and tanner, and Benjamin Hawes,
gentleman. They divided the building,
and Putnam's half included this room. In
1815 he installed the block-printed scenic
wallpaper, *Paysage Indien,* the work of
Joseph Dufour of Paris.

The vogue of pictorial wallpapers
began when Chinese examples were introduced to Europe and America in the
eighteenth century; throughout the following century, the French led the industry. In 1804 French manufacturers began
producing panoramas, or scenic wallpapers, such as the St. Louis example, made
of vertical strips of paper joined together
to form a continuous scene around the
room. *Paysage Indien* depicts a tiger hunt
and dancing figures; the jungle landscape
is embellished with temples of southern
India alongside a Mughal fort of northern India.

Claret Jug, 1870–1880
English
Design attributed to Frederick E. Kny,
Bohemian, active 1870–1920
Manufactured by Thomas Webb and
Sons, English, 1837–1964
Glass
Height: 11¹³/₁₆ in. (30 cm.)
Purchase: Friends Fund 16:1989

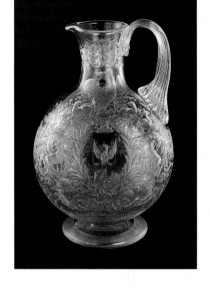

Rock-crystal carving is a style of wheel-engraving in which all the cut areas are polished, as are the uncut areas. It produces a more brilliant effect than other methods, and is often used over a larger part of the object's surface. The technique developed in England during the last two decades of the nineteenth century. Thomas Webb and Sons, one of the most influential English glass firms of the period, specialized in rock-crystal engraved glass. Frederick E. Kny, a Bohemian craftsman, was a leading engraver with the firm.

Minton Factory, English, 1796–present
Vase, 1878
Stoke-on-Trent
Porcelain
Height: 15¾ in. (40.1 cm.)
Gift of Mrs. Leonard Rakow in memory
of her husband, Dr. Leonard S. Rakow
90:1989

The Minton Factory gained an international reputation in the second half of the nineteenth century for its high-quality porcelains, many the handiwork of foreign artists. Through the expertise of these workers, Minton became one of the few companies which produced the painstaking, time-consuming, and expensive *pâte-sur-pâte,* or body-on-body, wares.

   The *pâte-sur-pâte* method originated at the Sèvres factory in France, inspired by Chinese vases. Louis-Marc-Emmanuel Solon introduced it to Minton in 1870. This vase is typical of his pieces at the Paris Exhibition of 1878.

Cabinet, c. 1865
English
Designed by Charles Bevan
Manufactured by Marsh and Jones
Satinwood and various wood inlays
Height: 58¼ in. (148 cm.)
Purchase: Friends' Fund 86:1990

This High Victorian cabinet, designed by
Charles Bevan and manufactured by
Marsh & Jones in Leeds, England, was
among the furnishings provided to Titus
Salt, Jr., of Baildon Lodge, in preparation
for his wedding in early 1866. Other
items in the suite included a piano and
ottoman, which were illustrated and
described in a period publication, *The
Building News.* The piano survives at
Lotherton Hall, England. An extensive
bill of sale dated 1866 from Marsh and
Jones mentions the cabinet, and a label
from the firm is still attached to the back
of the piece.

The satinwood piece is decorated
with intricate designs inlaid in dark and
light woods such as purplewood, amboy-
na, and harewood. The interior of the
fall-front is fitted with sliding trays of
ash; the cupboards are lined with blue
silk velvet; and the mounts are lacquered
brass. The inlay motifs probably were
inspired by exotic examples in the classic
Victorian pattern body by Owen Jones,
The Grammer of Ornament.

Bevan was a well-known Victorian
craftsman. He advertised as a "medieval
cabinet maker" and "alternatively as a
medieval designer." His designs employ
trefoils and pointed arches as decorative
motifs, characteristic of the Gothic
Revival or Reformed Gothic style.

■

Pottier and Stymus, American, 1859–1888
Side Chair, 1865–1875
Walnut, brass, velvet
Height: 38⅞ in. (98.6 cm.)
Purchase: Funds given by Mr. and Mrs.
Stanley F. Jackes and Donors to the 1985
Annual Appeal 82:1986.1

Designers emigrating from France and
Germany in the nineteenth century
brought to America current European
styles and traditions of excellent craftsmanship. French artisans August Pottier,
a cabinetmaker, and William Pierre
Stymus, an upholsterer, began their
American careers in the 1840s with the
New York firm of Rochefort and Skarren.
They became foremen of their respective
sections before taking over the company
in 1859 and transforming it into Pottier
and Stymus, one of the leading furniture-
making and decorating concerns of the
late nineteenth century. At its peak, the
business employed 700 workmen and

manufactured furniture in the full range
of revival styles popular at the time,
including the Renaissance Revival represented by this pair of chairs.

The original parlor set was comprised
of a sofa, side chairs, an armchair, and a
curule (an armchair with low back). The
present show-cover reproduces the original red silk velvet upholstery, fragments
of which survived on one chair. Nearly
all the original underupholstery and
tufting pattern remain on both chairs,
providing unusually complete documentation.

■

John La Farge, American, 1835–1910
Pair of Windows: **Hollyhocks** and
Flowering Cherry Tree and Peony,
1882
Stained glass
Each: 87¼ x 37¼ in. (221.6 x 94.6 cm.)
Purchase: Funds given by the Decorative
Arts Society in honor of the Twentieth
Anniversary of the Friends of The Saint
Louis Art Museum 31:1972.1,.2

These windows were conceived and
crafted for architect John Sturgis's rede-
sign of the Frederick Lothrop Ames
house in Boston's Back Bay, during the
period in La Farge's career when he was
most actively involved not only in design
for stained glass, but in all phases of its
manufacture. La Farge was a great inno-
vator, and in these windows he mixed

opalescent, molded, rough-cut, and fused
elements to achieve a brilliant play of
light and shadow, rich colors, and a complex decorative scheme. The subject and
composition of the designs reflect the
artist's interest in the exotic and the influence of Japanese prints.

In addition to working in glass, La
Farge was a painter in oils and watercolor,
a muralist, an innovative illustrator, and
a designer of extraordinary decorative
programs for ecclesiastical and domestic
interiors. These windows originally
flanked the fireplace on the landing of
the Grand Stairhall of the Ames house;
two others from the same commission
are now in the National Museum of
American Art in Washington, D.C.

■

Tiffany and Company, American,
New York, 1853–present
Punch Bowl, 1886
Designed by Edward C. Moore,
American, 1827–1891
Silver
Diameter: 15 in. (38.1 cm.)
Anonymous Gift 452:1979

The custom of presenting silver objects
to commemorate events or to recognize
services and accomplishments is as old as
silversmithing itself. During the nineteenth century, presentation silver was
most often the gift of a group to an individual, intended as a showy demonstration of respect and gratitude. The punch
bowl, a traditional form for presentation
silver in earlier centuries, continued to be
a favorite, symbolizing a successful life-
style and the achievement of wealth and
power.

This large punch bowl was presented
by employees of the Anheuser-Busch
Brewery in St. Louis to Lilly Anheuser
Busch and Adolphus Busch on their
twenty-fifth wedding anniversary. As this
was also the silver anniversary of the
firm, the event was particularly meaning-
ful to the employees. The concept for the
bowl was developed by Edward C.
Moore, chief designer at Tiffany and
Company from 1868 to 1891, and is characteristic of his work. Moore typically
chose ornamental motifs specific to the
occasion of the presentation; in this case
he used beer kegs draped with hop vines
and barley to decorate the bowl.

Edward C. Moore was the son of
John C. Moore, a leading New York City
silversmith whom Tiffany and Company
hired in 1851. Following the father's re-
tirement in 1853, the firm selected his
equally talented son as his replacement.
The younger Moore's highly successful
career with Tiffany lasted forty years. As
both designer and business manager, he
was responsible for most of the innovations and success of the company following the Civil War.

Side Chair, 1895–1904
Italian, Milan
Designed by Carlo Bugatti, Italian,
1856–1940
Wood, parchment, brass, silk
Height: 58⅝ in. (149 cm.)
Purchase: Funds given in memory of
Alfred Landesman and Museum
Purchase 68:1979

Carlo Bugatti's strikingly original furniture relies on a combination of unorthodox materials and imaginative motifs inspired by the Near and Far East; the influence of Moorish art is particularly pronounced. Though related to the international Art Nouveau tendencies at the turn of the century, his eclecticism, complex construction, and individuality are distinctive.

Following his training as an architect at the Brera School in Milan and the Beaux-Arts Academy in France, Bugatti turned to the design of furniture. His early work drew on historical precedents, gradually evolving into bolder and more inventive forms, and finally taking on highly sculptural, serpentine qualities.

This side chair is typical of Bugatti's work between the 1890s and 1904, a period in which he used vellum as an upholstery material and decorated his furniture with a variety of abstract geometric inlays of colored metals and woods. Circles and sections of circles dominated his designs at the time. Japanese-inspired painted ornament, as on the back of this chair, and silk tassel fringes also were common features. Though idiosyncratic, Bugatti's creative legacy inspired his sons Rembrandt, a sculptor, and Ettore, an automobile designer.

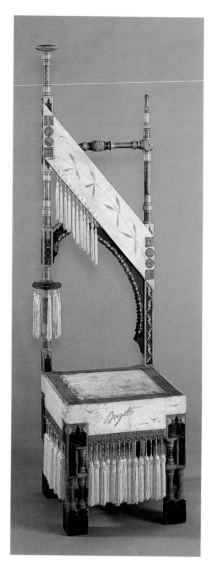

Dining Chair, designed 1901
Designed by Frank Lloyd Wright,
American, 1867–1959
Manufactured by John W. Ayers
Company, American, Chicago, 1887–1914
Oak
Height: 55⅞ in. (141.9 cm.)
Purchase: Funds given by the Decorative
Arts Society 239:1977

Frank Lloyd Wright was one of the
founders of the Prairie School, a style
modeled to fit the broad expanses of the
Midwest terrain. Prairie School buildings,
generally single-family residences, were
strongly horizontal with heavy sheltering
roofs.

Many of Wright's residential commissions included furnishings as well. The
furniture tended to be architectural in
scale, and often was fashioned from the
same wood as the paneling of the house
for which it was intended. The key to
Wright's design was an insistence on
simplicity, achieved through the use of
rigid geometric forms and refined proportions, and a commitment to creating
forms appropriate for human use. He
opposed the strict adherence to hand-
crafting methods of construction then
advocated by the mainstream Arts and
Crafts movement, embracing instead the
use of machine technology if the furniture was designed properly.

This dining chair is part of a set made
for the Ward W. Willits house, completed
in 1902 in Highland Park, Illinois. When
grouped, the high-backed chairs create a
sense of enclosure and intimacy, and
suggest the formality of dining. Wright
developed this basic style, with turned
spindles, for his own dining room chairs
in 1895, and reused it more than any
other of his furniture designs. The chair
has no historical precedent, but did
influence subsequent furniture designers.

Gorham Manufacturing Company,
American, 1831–present
Ewer and Plateau, 1903
Designed by William C. Codman, active
at Gorham 1891–1914
Silver
Ewer height: 19⅜ in. (49.2 cm.)
Plateau diameter: 12⅝ in. (32 cm.)
Purchase: Funds given by the Harry
Edison Foundation and the Rose J. Jonas
Bequest 823:1983

In reaction to the low quality of ma-
chine-made products, the English Arts
and Crafts movement of the 1880s and
1890s advocated a return to hand craftsmanship. The ideals of the movement
were quickly adopted in America by
many factories, including the Gorham
Manufacturing Company. Although
mechanization had contributed signifi-
cantly to the success of Gorham, in 1896
the firm decided to produce a line of
handcrafted wares. Three conditions
were set for production of these pieces:
the hammer was to be the primary tool;
the designer and craftsman were to work
together as closely as possible; and the
final product was to be identifiable with
its own century. In this last point,
Gorham differed from Arts and Crafts
silversmiths fashioning wares in styles
revived or derivative from earlier periods.

Gorham formally introduced its
handcrafted line at the 1900 Paris International Exposition as Martele, the
French word for hand-hammered, a
name meant to imply quality and exclu-
sivity. Martele was a purer alloy than the
usual sterling quality, and most items in
the line were unique designs made to
special order.

As was typical of Martele, at least two
craftsmen worked on this set. Gorham's
plant log indicates the silversmith spent
80 hours and the chaser spent 126 hours
on the ewer alone. Hand-polishing ensured that the hammer marks remained
visible, and Martele was originally oxi-
dized with sulfides to highlight details of
the decoration.

Adelaide Alsop Robineau, American,
1865–1929
University City Pottery, American,
1910–1914
Vases, 1910–1914
University City, Missouri
Porcelain
Heights range from 9½ to 6⅛ in.
(24.2 to 15.6 cm.)
Bequest of Elsa K. Bertig in memory of
Joseph and Elsa Bertig, by exchange
471, 472, 473:1979
Purchase: Friends Fund 215:1980

The University City Pottery grew out of
the American Women's League, founded
in St. Louis in 1907 by publisher Edward
Gardner Lewis. Lewis hired contemporary ceramic artists to teach at the Pottery and produce exhibition-quality pieces. Taxile Doat, a famous French ceram-
ist, was brought in as director, a post he
held throughout the firm's short life.

After the closing of the American Wom-
en's League in 1911, many artists left the
Pottery, and Doat reorganized it as the
University City Porcelain Works.

Doat was known in France and in
this country for his mastery of glazing
techniques. Most famous are his delicate
crystalline glazes, fired at very high tem-
peratures to create crystals of varying
sizes across the body of the ceramic.
Another artist active at the University
City Pottery who explored glazes was
Adelaide Robineau. She began potting in
Syracuse, New York, about 1903. During
her year-long stay in Missouri in 1910 she
created dramatic variegated effects. Significant works by Doat, Robineau, and
other University City artists received
awards and recognition at several international expositions, and continue to
serve as models to ceramists today.

MR-534 Armchair, designed 1927
Designed by Ludwig Mies van der Rohe,
German, 1886–1969
Nickel-plated tubular steel, horsehair,
ebonized wood
Height: 30½ in. (77.4 cm.)
Purchase: Museum Shop Funds 53:1987

In the first decades of the twentieth
century, architecture and interior design
responded to the influence of industry
and the development of new materials.
Mies van der Rohe, in the MR series of
chair designs from 1926–1927, experimented with cantilevered construction
and the use of continuous curved tubular
steel. The challenge of cantilevering was
to modify traditional chair forms and
eliminate the rear legs, thereby allowing
the chair to expose its relationship to the
seated human body. This radical redefini-
tion was possible due to the capacity of
tubular steel to take weight and stress.

Mies was granted a patent for cantilevered tubular steel chairs in 1927, and his
MR designs remain in production today.

Mies van der Rohe was a founding
father of modern architecture. He
trained with noted designers Bruno Paul
and Peter Behrens, and joined the Deut-
scher Werkbund, an organization established in 1907 to improve the quality of
industrial design in Germany. He was a
colleague of architects Walter Gropius
and Le Corbusier, and from 1930–1933
served as the last director of the Bauhaus.
In 1938, Mies emigrated to the United
States, bringing the principles of the
International Style to American architecture.

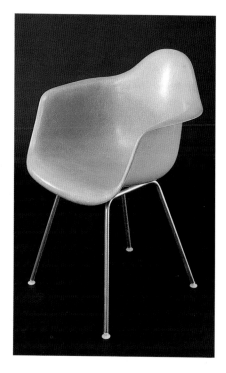

LCW [Low Chair Wood], 1946
Designed by Charles Eames, American,
1907–1978
Manufactured by Herman Miller, Inc.,
American, 1923–present
Plywood
Height: 27 in. (68.5 cm.)
Gift of David A. Hanks 146:1976

Armchair, 1950
Designed by Charles Eames, American,
1907–1978
Manufactured by Herman Miller, Inc.,
American, 1923–present
Polyester fiberglass
Height: 30¾ in. (78.1 cm.)
Gift of Mrs. Charles Lorenz 124:1984

Charles Eames, a native of St. Louis, is
considered the first American Modernist
designer to have energetically embraced
machine technology for furniture production. Throughout his career, Eames
approached design as a problem to be
solved as inexpensively and directly as

advanced methods allowed. His furniture
designs are the result of repeated studies
of the human form and its dimensions.

Eames worked in diverse fields, including architecture and film, yet his
greatest fame derives from furniture. His
first chair designs utilized the strength of
molded wood; their success resulted from
Eames's technical innovation of curving
thin laminated veneers in more than one
direction on the same piece. Additionally, to avoid marring the surface appearance with joinery, Eames took advantage
of a recently developed welding system to
secure rubber disks as joints between the
molded wood sections.

Eames also experimented with fiberglass, a molded polyester used for its high
resistance to impact and weather. The
chairs resulting from these experiments
were eminently suitable for mass
production.

Dwight Dillon, American, 1918–1959
Chalice, 1958
Silver
Height: 10⅝ in. (27 cm.)
Mark: (small D overlapping larger D)
Purchase: Funds given by the Decorative
Arts Society in honor of Lynn E. Springer
65:1981

Considered one of St. Louis's finest silversmiths, Dwight Dillon first became
interested in metalworking while serving
as an aircraft mechanic with the Air
Force in 1942. Dillon's designs for liturgical silver won him commissions from
both Protestant and Catholic churches.
He considered this piece the embodi-
ment of the essence of a chalice. He
raised the base and stem from a single
piece of silver, a time-consuming process
on this scale. The proportions of the
piece depart from the traditional formula
for a chalice: the stem is taller, and the
cup is smaller.

Maria Regnier, American, born 1901
Coffee Service, 1945–1950
St. Louis
Silver
Coffeepot height: 8⅝ in. (22 cm.)
Mark (each): MR (conjoined in rectan-
gle) HANDWROUGHT STERLING
Gift of Mr. John Goodman 22:1989.1–.4

Maria Regnier received a degree in Art
Education from Washington University
in St. Louis, Missouri, where she became
interested in metalworking. Her works
were primarily unique commissions,
usually for friends and family members.
Regnier's pieces rely on shape and high-
quality craftsmanship for their appeal.
Her confident use of thick sheets of silver
further contributed to her success. Although Regnier had little contact with
national and international artists, her
sense of design and proportion was consistent with contemporary trends of the
Bauhaus and Scandinavian workshops.

■

Wendell Castle, American, born 1932
Music Stand, designed 1963,
manufactured 1980
Scottsville, New York
White oak, rosewood
Height: 55 in. (139.7 cm.)
Purchase: National Endowment for the
Arts, Anonymous Matching Funds, and
Matching Funds given by Grace Morris
Williamson and Alice P. Francis 93:1982

Wendell Castle is an artist whose creations
deliberately challenge the traditional
utilitarian function of furniture. Castle's
background as a sculptor is clearly dis-
cernible in his sensitive, organic use of
laminated wood carved into furniture-
like forms. He dissolves the boundaries
between craft and art, and his products
exhibit a high degree of workmanship.

In addition to recognizable and
usable forms such as this music stand,
Castle pursues surrealistic effects in semi-
functional artifacts. Carved clothing and
other object shapes are integrated into
such pieces.

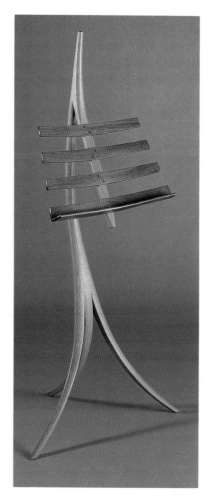

Prints,
Drawings,
and
Photographs

■

Albrecht Dürer, German, 1471–1528
St. Eustace, c.1501
Engraving
13⅞ x 10⅜ in. (35.6 x 26.6 cm.)
Purchase 255:1916

Painter, printmaker, designer of stained glass and metalwork, and theoretician, Albrecht Dürer possessed a combination of artistic genius and self-awareness that made him one of the outstanding figures in the history of German art. Dürer is unsurpassed as a printmaker. Both in woodcut and in engraving he achieved an unprecedented monumentality and dramatic effect, learned from Italian Renaissance art, with a northern love of detail.

St. Eustace, the largest of Dürer's engravings, illustrates the Saint's conversion to Christianity upon witnessing the vision of a stag with a crucifix between its horns. Dürer's tapestry-like composition consists of a rich variety of tiny engraved lines that create a shimmering surface. His command of the highly demanding and meticulous art of engraving is most evident in his remarkable ability to translate onto the metal plate subtle variations in light and texture, and a wealth of details all organized into a monumental whole.

Giorgio Vasari so admired Dürer's large engravings, *St. Eustace* and *Large Fortune,* that he explained them as the artist's effort to surpass his Netherlandish contemporary Lucas van Leyden "in quantity as well as in quality." Dürer himself thought very highly of this print, selling and giving away many impressions of it during his journey to the Netherlands in 1520.

■
Ugo da Carpi, Italian, c.1480–c.1532
Diogenes, c.1527
Chiaroscuro woodcut
Sheet: 18¹⁵/₁₆ x 13¾ in. (48.1 x 35 cm.)
Purchase: The Sidney S. and Sadie
Cohen Print Purchase Fund 23:1984

Ugo da Carpi's chiaroscuro woodcut
Diogenes, based on a drawing by the
Italian Mannerist Parmigianino, is considered to be not only the artist's masterpiece, but also one of the prime examples
of this technique. The St. Louis impres-
sion is beautifully executed in blue-gray
matte inks, regarded by scholars to be
indicative of the earliest examples. The
effects of this technique were achieved
through the use of multiple blocks,
printed in overlapping fashion. Whether

Ugo da Carpi should be credited with
the invention of the method is open to
debate; however, the importance of his
artistic achievement is unquestionable,
as witnessed by the quality of his cutting
and the complexity of the tonal separa-
tions.

The subject of the print is the Greek
Cynic philosopher Diogenes, famous for
his eccentricities. According to legend,
when Plato defined man as a featherless
biped, Diogenes ridiculed him by producing a plucked rooster and exclaiming:
"This is the Platonic man!"

■

Augustin Hirschvogel, German, 1503–1553
**River Landscape with Large Tree at
Left,** 1546
Etching
Sheet: 5½ x 7⅞ in. (14 x 20 cm.)
Purchase: Friends Fund and Gift of
J. Lionberger Davis, by exchange 19:1988

This etching by Augustin Hirschvogel is
representative of the Danube School
style, which flourished along the Danube
River from Regensburg to Vienna in the
early sixteenth century. The movement
introduced landscape and the depiction
of nature as dominant compositional
elements, reflecting a close relationship
between man and his surroundings.
The Danube School originated with the
work of Lucas Cranach the Elder,
Albrecht Altdorfer, and Wolf Huber, who
were strongly influenced by Albrecht
Dürer. Hirschvogel, considered one of
the leaders of the second generation of
Danube School artists, was a glass painter, mathematician, and cartographer.
During the last ten years of his career, he
produced more than 300 etchings, primarily illustrations for books. Among
these was a group of thirty-five independent landscape etchings which revealed a
poetic and romantic aspect of his work.

  River Landscape with Large Tree at Left
is characteristic of Hirschvogel's early
compositional style, with the large tree in
the foreground, the village and architectural details in the middle ground, and
the mountain range in the distance. He
often used a winding river to draw the
viewer's eye into the scene. Moss-laden
trees, characteristic of Altdorfer, and the
loose loops of foliage, reminiscent of
Huber, are incorporated into Hirschvogel's intimate and gentle view of nature.

Jean-Auguste-Dominique Ingres, French,
1780–1867
John Russell, Sixth Duke of Bedford,
1815
Graphite
15¼ x 11⅜ in. (38.6 x 28.9 cm.)
Purchase 354:1952

It has been said that ever since the time
of Holbein, the English had not sat for
so great a portraitist as Ingres. This keenly observed portrait of John Russell, sixth
Duke of Bedford (1766–1839) was one of
many superb drawings of wealthy En-
glishmen on The Grant Tour that Ingres
executed during his sojourn in Rome
from 1806–1820. Here the fine graphite
lines that he uses to render the physiog-
nomy capture the sitter's strength of
character. A proponent of reform of the
British Parliament and a long-time member of the Society of Friends of the People, the Duke of Bedford also wrote a
series of books on the natural sciences.
He is shown here as a man of letters
holding a book in his right hand and
resting his left arm on a table with his
writing implements.

Ingres's portrait drawings remind one
of his admiration for the classical and
High Renaissance traditions in art and
his faith in the primacy of line over color.
He wrote of his adoration of "Raphael
and his century; the ancients, and above
all the divine Greeks; in music Gluck,
Mozart, and Haydn."

Francisco Goya y Lucientes, Spanish, 1746–1828
Modo de Volar (A Way of Flying), c.1816–1820
Etching and aquatint
Plate: 9½ x 13¾ in. (24.4 x 35 cm.)
Purchase: The Sidney and Sadie Cohen Foundation, Inc. Print Purchase Fund 7:1968

Francisco Goya, considered one of the finest *peintre-graveurs,* did not begin making prints until late in his career, after he was left completely deaf by an illness in 1793. Goya's print series often rival the significance and emotional intensity of his paintings from the same time.

This etching bridges Goya's last two series of prints. Although issued posthumously with the series *Los Disparates,* it is now considered the concluding plate to *La Tauromaquía* of 1816. *Modo de Volar* is one of the trial proofs printed in approximately 1848; the regular edition was not published until 1864. It is an apt conclusion to a series that depicts the valor of the matadors and the energy of the bullfight. From the ominously murky sky appear fantastic bird-like machines that carry men in flight. This enigmatic imagery suggests that just as man has conquered the wild bull through skill, knowledge, and courage, so one day will he conquer the sky.

Edouard Manet, French, 1832–1883
The Races, 1864–1865
Lithograph
Image: 15¼ x 20 in. (38.6 x 51 cm.)
Bequest of Horace M. Swope 643:1940

This lithograph often has been referred to as the first Impressionist print. Manet's unconventional, head-on composition leaves a dramatic void in the center, drawing the viewer's eye into the picture by means of strong diagonal lines. These elements, combined with rapid, sketch-like strokes, instill the scene with a sense of movement and great energy. One can almost hear the thundering hooves of the horses and the cheers emanating from the grandstand.

Prints served many purposes for Manet. Often based on painted compositions, his etchings and lithographs were a means to reach a wide audience. He looked to his contemporaries, as well as to earlier artists such as Rembrandt and Goya, for inspiration.

It is difficult to date this work exactly, since Manet dated very few of his prints. It relates, however, to several works in other media ranging from 1865 to 1872, and we know that it was published posthumously in 1884 in an edition of a hundred prints.

Paul Gauguin, French, 1848–1903
L'Esprit Moderne et le Catholicisme,
1897–1898
Manuscript, transfer drawings in black,
and woodcuts
12⅝ x 7⅛ in. (32 x 18 cm.)
Gift of Vincent L. Price, Jr., in memory
of his parents, Marguerite and Vincent L.
Price 287:1948

L'Esprit Moderne et le Catholicisme
(Catholicism and the Modern Mind)
was written by Gauguin in Tahiti in 1897
and 1898, and transcribed by him in its
present form in Atuana, Marquesas
Islands, in 1902. Gauguin wrote ten trea-
tises on subjects ranging from art and
religion to personal insights about the
modern world.

   This text is a treatise on religion, a
subject on which Gauguin was well-read;
in it Gauguin criticizes the efforts of the
Catholic Church to convert the South
Seas natives whom Gauguin considered
beautiful and godlike. The front and
back covers are adorned with transfer
drawings, while the inside covers reveal
two woodcuts. Gauguin's choice of illustrations for the outside covers, which
apparently were conceived as a pair, reflects the religious theme of the text. The
front cover represents the "brothel" of
the Magdalene, and the back cover depicts the Nativity. Two earlier handprint-
ed woodcuts have been applied to the
inside covers: *Soyez amoureuses, vous serez
heureuses* (Be in Love, You Will Be
Happy) and *Women, Animals, and Foliage,* inscribed in pen and ink – Paradis
perdu – (Paradise Lost).

Vincent van Gogh, Dutch, 1853–1890
**Fishing Boats at
Saintes-Maries-de-la-Mer,** 1888
Reed pen and brown ink and graphite on
wove paper
9½ x 12½ in. (24.3 x 31.9 cm.)
Gift of Mr. and Mrs. Joseph Pulitzer, Jr.
137:1984

The climax of van Gogh's brief, ten-year
period of artistic activity is often considered to have been his fifteen-month stay
in Arles from February 1888 to May 1889.
During the sojourn, van Gogh completed some 200 paintings and over 100
drawings. *Fishing Boats at Saintes-Maries-
de-la-Mer,* which dates from this time,
belongs to a group of works executed
during and after a week-long visit to that
Mediterranean village thirty miles from
Arles.

Van Gogh finished three paintings
and nine drawings while in Saintes-
Maries-de-la-Mer; on his return to Arles,

however, he completed thirty-two additional drawings after his own paintings.
The St. Louis sheet is one of two drawings after the painting *Seascape at Saintes-
Maries-de-la-Mer,* now in the Rijksmuse-
um in Amsterdam. The artist translated
the composition of the painting, with its
piled on strokes of bright color, into
swiftly executed drawings of the greatest
expressive economy. Far from being labo-
rious copies, the drawings display great
freedom of execution. The lines are varied and rhythmic. It was the artist's goal
at this time to allow his drawings to
become "more spontaneous, more exaggerated," a trait readily observed in this
lively and energetic sheet. In this way,
van Gogh emulated the Japanese who,
in his own words "draw quickly, very
quickly, like a lightning flash, because
their nerves are finer, their feeling
simpler."

■

Mary Cassatt, American, 1845–1926
Afternoon Tea Party, 1891
Drypoint and aquatint
13⅝ x 10½ in. (34.6 x 26.8 cm.)
Purchase and Funds donated by Mr.
and Mrs. Warren McK. Shapleigh,
Mrs. G. Gordon Hertslet and
Mrs. Richard I. Brumbaugh
4:1976

Mary Cassatt, the only American artist
included among the Impressionists,
is known primarily for her paintings
and pastels of women and children. She
began making prints relatively late in
her career and was greatly influenced by
the work of her fellow Impressionists
Edgar Degas and Camille Pissarro in this
medium.

Along with Degas and Pissarro, Cassatt played a decisive role in the revival of
printmaking, particularly etching, in the
nineteenth century, and artists such as
Degas, Pissarro, and Cassatt joined in the

excitement. The influence of Japanese
art, especially *ukiyo-e* prints, is evident in
the works of the period.

Cassatt's *Afternoon Tea Party* is one
of a group of ten prints executed by the
artist in 1891. These color prints are
considered by many to be her finest
work. They demonstrate not only her
masterful handling of complicated printing techniques, but also her application
of characteristics of Japanese art. These
are recognizable in the print's abstract
compositional quality, with its flattening
of forms, as well as the distinctive manner in which each print is inked. *Afternoon Tea Party* is the only color print to
which Cassatt consistently applied hand
touches, painting with gold the rims of
the cups and saucers and the hat of the
woman at the left.

■

Edgar Degas, French, 1834–1917
Ballet Dancers in the Wings, 1900
Pastel on paper
28 x 26 in. (71.1 x 66 cm.)
Purchase 24:1935

Degas's preference for figural subject matter over landscape is in stark contrast to much of the work of his Impressionist friends, such as Monet and Pissarro. In fact, Degas favored more manageable interior scenes and the effects of gaslight rather than working outdoors in the sunlight.

By 1874 Degas had established a reputation as a specialist in the depictions of the dancers of the opera theater; in fact, half of his mature work was devoted to this theme. *Ballet Dancers in the Wings* is a beautiful pastel from Degas's late period. It was his custom at this time to re-use figural compositions by making tracings, which preserved the original

and allowed him to explore and experiment with variations and reversals. Thus, the figures in this pastel appear in other works and are related to several drawings.

This composition of four dancers, two standing and two seated, arranged on a diagonal in descending height, is enlivened by the forceful line and vibrant, intense colors prevalent in this period of his career. The artist has moved his dancers off the stage, portraying them in the wings, in repose, weary from their intense efforts. Degas chose to depict not the celebrated dancers but the girls whom one contemporary called the "poor little plebians," with their angular, youthful bodies and broad, common features. Degas here prefers the confined spaces of backstage instead of the performances and rehearsal rooms of his earlier work.

■

Charles Sheeler, American, 1883–1965
Still Life (Suspended Forms), c.1922
Charcoal, chalk, and watercolor
19 x 15¼ in. (48.2 x 38.7 cm.)
Bequest of Marie Setz Hertslet 123:1972

Charles Sheeler was a pioneer of American Modernism. A gifted photographer as well as a painter and draughtsman, Sheeler was in close contact with Alfred Stieglitz and was admired by Edward Steichen, Paul Strand, and Edward Weston. While his choice of subject matter for *Suspended Forms,* a precisionist still life, appears traditional, his execution and intention were not. The deceptively simple arrangement was quite purposeful. Sheeler stated that his goal was to give his work "the absolute beauty we are accustomed to associate with objects suspended in a vacuum." As such, the Etruscan pitcher, glass tumbler, glass dish with marbles, and apple are removed from any recognizable context;

only a cursory line connotes the table top. The emphasis is on the structure of these elements, pure and abstract, with no indication of shadows.

Sheeler's photography informed his modernist explorations in drawing and painting. *Suspended Forms,* one of a group of six still lifes exhibited in 1922, is related to a photograph by Sheeler. While the photograph depicts the same elements, the artist has replaced the horizontal format of the photograph with the vertical orientation of the drawing, thus accentuating its abstract qualities and the individual nature of the various objects in space.

■

Charles Demuth, American, 1883–1935
Eggplant and Green Pepper, 1925
Watercolor with graphite
18 x 11⅞ in. (45.6 x 30.2 cm.)
Purchase: Eliza McMillan Purchase
Fund 2: 1948

As a watercolorist, Charles Demuth had
few equals. He found much of his inspiration in Cézanne's late watercolors,
devising ways to combine a formal organization with a developing interest in
geometric associations. While architectural scenes and landscapes had earlier
held his interest, in the late teens and
early 1920s he embarked on a series of
still lifes that focused on simple arrange-
ments of fruits, vegetables, and flowers.

In *Eggplant and Green Pepper* two
unassuming vegetables sit on a circular
woven surface with a simple glass jar
from whose mouth a single leaf casually
protrudes. The vegetables are rendered
with great sensitivity to the subtle irregu-
larities in their smooth and undulating
surfaces. Demuth's use of blotting technique and his practise of leaving portions
of the paper blank enhance and extend
the ethereal delicacy of the composition
as a whole.

Max Beckmann, German, 1884–1950
Self-Portrait, 1922
Woodcut
Sheet: 12¾ x 10 in. (32.4 x 25.3 cm.)
Purchase: Friends Fund 1796:1981

The self-portrait held a great fascination for Max Beckmann, one of Germany's most important artists of the twentieth century. This subject appears often in his paintings, prints, and drawings.

Unlike other German artists of his time, such as Ernst Ludwig Kirchner, Erich Heckel, and Emil Nolde, Beckmann executed few woodcuts, only eighteen in an oeuvre of over 300 prints. This striking work is the artist's only single-figure self-portrait in the woodcut technique, and is one of two known impressions of the image's second state. The forceful positioning of the figure on the sheet presents Beckmann as a successful, confident, well-respected artist, a position he enjoyed at the time of the print's completion.

Otto Dix, German, 1891–1969
Head of a Woman with a Bow, 1926
Charcoal and graphite
13¾ x 13 in. (35 x 33 cm.)
Purchase: Funds given by Mr. and Mrs.
Elmer Kiefer, McMillan-Avery Fund of
the St. Louis Community Foundation,
Mr. and Mrs. Eugene F. Williams, Jr.,
John R. Goodall Trust, Mr. and Mrs.
Jack Ansehl, and Mr. and Mrs. John D.
Cleator through the 1989 Annual Appeal
66:1990

Along with Max Beckmann and George
Grosz, Otto Dix was a representative
of the social realist tendency in German
art called "die Neue Sachlichkeit." This
magnificent drawing is a study for a
nearly life-size painting (Galerie der Stadt
Stuttgart) depicting three prostitutes
with all the brutality and acerbity expressed by the Neue Sachlichkeit artists
in their portrayals of contemporary
society.

The drawing is for the head of the
scrawny prostitute at the left of the
painting. The distorted face of the young
woman recalls Dix's artistic beginnings in
German Expressionism as well as his
affinity for his German Renaissance fore-
bears Matthias Grünewald and Hans
Baldung Grien. While the adept shading
of the powerful, solid head recalls the old
masters, the swift, spontaneous execution
is thoroughly modern.

Dix had fought at the front in World
War I, and his imagination was obsessed
by the suffering, horror, and misery of
reality. In works such as *Head of a Young
Woman with a Bow*, Dix evokes the an-
guished saints of Grünewald and the
frenzied witches of Baldung to condemn
the social and spiritual values of his own
era.

Henri Matisse, French, 1869–1954
Woman in Armchair, 1936
Charcoal on paper
21 x 15¹⁵/₁₆ in. (53.2 x 40.5 cm.)
Purchase: Friends Fund and Funds given
in memory of Miriam O'Malley 9:1953

As a painter, Henri Matisse is considered
the greatest colorist of his time. The
essence of his art, however, lies in the
beauty of his line. A master draftsman,
Matisse was interested in form rather
than content. Drawing was a constant
activity throughout his long career.

Woman in Armchair, based on a model
in a studio arrangement, is exemplary of
Matisse's drawing style. Like many of his
charcoal drawings, it illustrates his concern with spatial relationships and the

atmospheric play of light and shade; his
lively line creates volume and defines
pattern.

Matisse wrote and spoke eloquently
about his work. "My drawing is the most
direct and purest translation of my emotion. This is made possible by simplifica-
tion of media. I have the feeling that my
emotion expresses itself through the
medium of plastic writing. As soon as
my line – inspired, so to speak, with a
life of its own – has molded the light of
the empty sheet without destroying the
tender whiteness of the paper, I stop. I
can no longer add or change. The page is
written, no correction is possible."

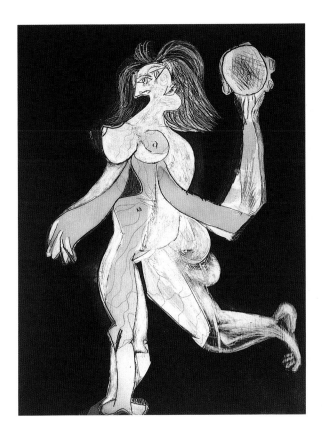

■
Pablo Picasso, Spanish, 1881–1973
Woman with Tambourine, 1938
Etching and aquatint
Plate: 26⅛ x 20¼ in. (66.5 x 51.3 cm.)
Gift of Joseph Pulitzer, Jr. 40:1952

Printmaking was a significant part of
Picasso's long and prolific career. His
interest in the medium emerged as he
matured and developed into one of the
major artistic forces in the twentieth
century. In addition to his paintings,
sculptures, drawings, and ceramics, he
created over 2,000 prints.

This unusually large print of *Woman
with Tambourine* is a technical achievement in aquatint; its overall uniformity
and richness are masterfully handled.
Picasso's talent as a draftsman is evident
in his skillful use of the scraper, the tool
actually employed to create the image
out of the darkness of the velvet-like
aquatint ground. Literally scraped onto
the plate and through the aquatint resin,
Picasso's haunting image of a Bacchante
figure emerges. The exaggerated proportions and vibrant presence of this figure
testify to Picasso's inventiveness and
talent as a master printmaker.

Jasper Johns, American, born 1930
Black and White Numerals: Figure 7,
1968
Lithograph
Sheet: 35 x 30 in. (88.8 x 76.3 cm.)
Purchase: Friends Fund 1976 34:1976.7

Jasper Johns has been a strong influence in the second half of the twentieth century. His paintings sometimes present an impenetrable mystery, inviting the viewer to ponder the enigmatic imagery and the complex vocabulary of symbols that seem to offer myriad possibilities of meaning.

Following the tradition of the painter-printmaker, Johns's work in lithography, etching, and screenprinting displays his constant desire to reshape ideas by reusing objects and subjects from his paintings, bronzes, or drawings.

Along with flags, targets, maps, and the alphabet, numbers have been a continuous subject for Johns. His *Black and White Numerals: Figures 0 to 9* are of such a scale as to compete with paintings. Johns emphasizes the individual character and feeling of each number within the group, with a definite sense of a beginning and an end. The surfaces of the prints are diverse and display Johns's tendency to mark the stone in a lively and inventive manner, manipulating wash and line to create a rich, luscious effect. In *Numeral 7*, a decal of the Mona Lisa has been transferred to the stone.

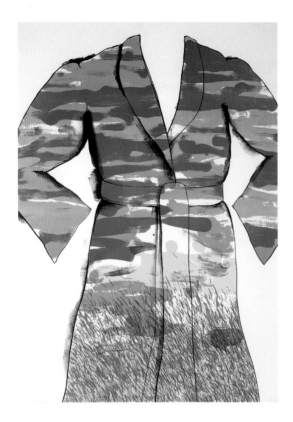

Jim Dine, American, born 1935
Self-Portrait: The Landscape, 1969
Color lithograph
Sheet: 53⅛ x 37⅝ in. (134.9 x 95.6 cm.)
Purchase: Funds given by Centerre
Bancorporation 39:1982

Along with Jasper Johns, Jim Dine has
been one of the major forces in contemporary printmaking. He has expanded
the traditional boundaries of the medium, employing unusual papers, hand
coloring, collage additions, and unexpected combinations of techniques.

In the early 1960s, Dine was active in
the Pop movement that sought to challenge the role of Abstract Expressionism.
His subjects – hearts, tools, palettes, and
robes – were highly symbolic and autobiographical. The robe theme emerged

from a group of paintings done at the
beginning of the 1960s. In those works,
as in *Self-Portrait: The Landscape,* the
robes seem to be worn by an invisible
man. As the title indicates, the robe – a
garment both formal and intimate – is
treated as a self-portrait. The artist uses
this unsettling image in multiple contexts, representing it in a wide range of
attitudes and settings.

■

Jacob Lawrence, American, born 1917
Builders #1, 1972
Watercolor and gouache over pencil
22½ x 30¾ in. (57.7 x 78.8 cm.)
Purchase: Eliza McMillan Fund 93:1972

Born and raised in New York's Harlem, Jacob Lawrence began his career in the 1930s, forging a personal style influenced by both contemporary Social Realism and colorful abstract composition. Lawrence frequently draws upon scenes of daily life in his urban surroundings, and a more general focus in much of his work has been the depiction of the struggles of life. Images of builders have been frequent in Lawrence's work since the early 1970s; they symbolize for him the aspirations and constructive capabilities of humanity.

In *Builders #1,* a powerful-looking man works in a studio strewn with colorful, geometrically formed tools, a scene that is presented close to the picture plane and therefore to the viewer. The stabilizing triangular form of Mount Rainier looms outside the window, an allusion to the artist's move to Seattle, Washington in 1971. Lawrence prefers to work with water-based media, and in this piece the gouache gives an opaque and flat character to the surface.

Jennifer Bartlett, American, born 1941
Black House, 1984
Pastel
26 x 40 in. (66 x 101.6 cm.)
Purchase: Eliza McMillan Purchase Fund
40:1985

Black House demonstrates Bartlett's fascination with the simple, geometric house form that appears in much of her work since the 1970s. This pastel depicts the ominous black structure deep within a densely foliated setting, alongside a creek flanked by a rowboat and a bridge. The drawing is one of a number of pieces Bartlett completed on the theme of the creek.

When Bartlett began to use oil pastel in 1983, her work took on a new richness of texture quite different from her earlier pieces painted on smooth, enameled surfaces. Much of her previous work was executed in direct response to Minimalist and Conceptual art; while she introduced simple recognizable images, she often utilized a grid system. This drawing marks a change in her approach. Bartlett continues to explore and create enigmatic imagery, but in a more painterly style, as witnessed in her sensuous handling of the surface and the wondrous inner light coming forth from the picture.

■

Charles Nègre, French, 1820–1880
Arles: Roman Ramparts, 1852
Salt print
9 x 12¾ in. (23 x 32.4 cm.)
Purchase: Museum Shop Fund 76:1989

Before turning to photography, Charles Nègre trained as a painter and was a student of Ingres and Delaroche. He initially used photography as an aid to his painting, but eventually dedicated himself to the medium.

While Nègre's early work in photography consisted of genre scenes, he soon became thoroughly immersed in the field of architectural images. In 1852 he began a most ambitious project: to photograph the monuments, archaeological ruins, and scenery of his birthplace, the Midi region of France. *Arles: Roman Ramparts* belongs to this project, which was never fully realized. The artist's intention was to depict the romantic atmosphere and picturesque quality of the Midi and not concern himself with documenting structures and monuments which were neglected and subject to vandalism. Nègre's photographs from this time, with their use of deep shadows and sunlight, reflect his sophisticated eye and pure photographic vision, rarely seen in images from such an early date.

Carleton E. Watkins, American,
1829–1916
**The Lyell Group, 13,191 Feet Above Sea
and Nevada Fall from Sentinel Dome
No. 96,** 1866
Albumen print
15³⁄₁₆ x 20⅜ in. (38.7 x 51.8 cm.)
Purchase 127:1977

Carleton E. Watkins was one of the most
celebrated landscape photographers of
the American West. His realization that
photography was an art form as well as a
useful tool of documentation freed him
to take advantage of nineteenth-century
land surveys while addressing the Romantic aesthetics of painting and literature at the time.

The Lyell Group, a mammoth plate
from 1866, was made when Watkins
accompanied a government-sponsored
geological survey party to the high areas
surrounding the Yosemite Valley.
Watkins approached the land with an
exhilarated self-confidence instilled by
his previous expeditions into the Valley.
This view shows the strong formal concerns of his mature style. The dark foreground recedes into the middleground
and background, which then culminates
in the gentle undulation of the horizon
line.

Paul Strand, American, 1890–1976
Church, Ranchos de Taos, New Mexico,
1931
Silver print
4⅞ x 5⅞ in. (11.8 x 15 cm.)
Purchase 74:1978

Paul Strand's early interest in photography coincided with the initial wave of Modernism in American visual arts. He sought to make "straight," unmanipulated images that combined the intrinsic capabilities of the photographic medium with objective reality.

Between 1930 and 1932, Strand made a series of photographs in New Mexico. Turning his camera to the rugged landscape and indigenous architecture, he strove to capture the essence of that mysterious region. *Church, Ranchos de Taos, New Mexico* exemplifies the purity of Strand's vision: by concentrating on its surface texture, Strand reveals the fundamental, organic nature of the building.

Walker Evans, American, 1903–1975
Allie May Burroughs, Wife of a Cotton Sharecropper, Hale County, Alabama,
1936
Silver print
9⅜ x 7½ in. (23.9 x 19.2 cm.)
Purchase: Bequest of Jean F. Harris and Funds given by Mr. and Mrs. Robert Rosenheim 146:1987

Walker Evans's straightforward style is evident in his famous portrait of an Alabama sharecropper's wife. Images such as this documented the plight of Depression-era America in hopes of motivating social and economic reforms. Evans approached his subject matter, be it tenant farmer, building, billboard, or subway portrait, as the lucid description of significant fact. A reader of nineteenth-century French novelist Gustave Flaubert, he believed artists should be invisible, but all-powerful.

■

Alexander Rodchenko, Russian,
1891–1956
Woman with a Camera, 1930s
Silver print
8 x 11⅜ in. (20.4 x 28.8 cm.)
Purchase: Funds given in honor of
Mary-Edgar Patton 21:1986

Alexander Rodchenko began his career
as a painter, exhibiting works with
Russian Supremitist and Constructivist
artists such as Vladimir Tatlin, Kasimir
Malevitch, and Liubov Popova. By the
early 1920s he was using photographs in
conjunction with his photomontages.

Rodchenko's photographs display an
underlying Modernist approach to the
medium – that of using photography to
express ideas in a form that is purely its
own and not an attempt to imitate painting. His images of everyday scenes are
taken from unexpected angles which
challenge conventional perspectives. In
Woman with a Camera, Rodchenko
shoots from above, accentuating the way
in which the camera's eye flattens the
composition and foreshortens the figure.
The dynamism thus achieved is heightened by the striking use of diagonals in
the tilted posture of the woman, the
stripes on her dress, and the planks of
wood on the ground. It was not Rodchenko's aim merely to convey information with his photographs, but rather to
have them function as the means for a
psychological response to a new era.

■

Ansel Adams, American, 1902–1984
Clearing Winter Storm,
Yosemite Valley, 1944
Silver print
10½ x 13¼ in. (26.5 x 33.7 cm.)
Purchase 62:1945

Ansel Adams is perhaps the best-known photographer of the twentieth century. While his work includes portraits, still lifes, and architectural photographs, he is primarily recognized for his images of the Western landscape. His lifelong association with the Sierra Nevada and its preservation began in 1916, when at the age of fourteen he made his first visit. Trained as a concert pianist, Adams turned to photography full time in 1930.

He was one of the founding members of Group f/64, photographers dedicated to the sharply focused image.

Adams's emotional involvement with his landscape subjects is apparent in his elegant depiction of *Clearing Winter Storm, Yosemite Valley.* Ever the flawless technician, Adams transcends mere description of a scene and strives to capture the elusive quality of light as it envelops the landscape. The result is a photograph translated into precise tonal harmony.

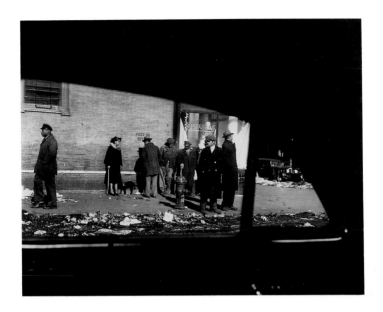

Gordon Parks, American, born 1912
Untitled, 1963
Silver print
10⅜ x 13¼ in. (26.2 x 33.7 cm.)
Purchase: Funds given by Mr. and Mrs.
Daniel L. Schlafly 197:1989

Although known primarily as a documentary photographer, Gordon Parks is an accomplished writer, musician, and filmmaker as well. In 1942 he was awarded a fellowship to study with Roy Stryker at the Farm Security Administration (FSA), where he came in contact with other photographers such as Walker Evans, Dorothea Lange, and Russell Lee. The only African-American photographer in the FSA, Parks traveled throughout the country, witnessing first-hand the effects of the Depression. He continued to work with Stryker at the Office of War Information, and later as a member of a seven-man team hired by Standard Oil Company of New Jersey to document American life at mid-century.

Parks is perhaps best known for his numerous photographic essays for *Life* magazine, where he was a full-time staff photographer from 1948 to 1961. While his subjects vary from Harlem street gangs to Winston Churchill and the civil rights movement, his ultimate focus and passion are people and the intimate details of daily life.

American

Painting

and Sculpture

John Singleton Copley, American,
1738–1815

Thaddeus Burr, 1758–1760
Oil on canvas
50⅝ x 39⅞ in. (128.6 x 101.3 cm.)
Purchase 174:1951

Eunice Dennie Burr, 1758–1760
Oil on canvas
49¹⁵⁄₁₆ x 39⅜ in. (126.9 x 100.1 cm.)
Purchase 173:1951

These works represent a high point
of American colonial portraiture, a field
dominated by John Singleton Copley
during the period between 1753 and 1774
when Copley left for England. Copley
was virtually a self-taught artist since
eighteenth-century Boston offered few
masters to serve as artistic models. His
first works were completed when he was
only fifteen, and by the late 1750s Copley
had achieved a style of compelling naturalism and sumptuous surface texture
evident in this pair of portraits.

Thaddeus Burr was a Fairfield, Con-
necticut landholder and a graduate of
Princeton. He was a close friend of John
Hancock, and was one of two Fairfield

delegates to the convention in Hartford to ratify the Constitution of 1788. Burr's hip-shot pose and clean, chiseled features reflect the rational ideology of the eighteenth century. His stance looks to America's political future: leaning against a classical relief, the allegorical figure of abundance makes reference both to his position as landholder as well as the Greek democratic ideals which soon would shape the ideologies of the American and French revolutions. In 1759 he married Eunice Dennie; the marriage may have been the occasion for the commission of these portraits.

Eunice Burr's portrait, dominated by the rich rose coloration of her dress and the ivory tones of the Mechlin lace at her sleeves and neckline, serves as a counterpoint to the satiny blue waistcoat her husband wears. The accomplished treatment of fabric displayed in both portraits looks ahead to Copley's later success in England. Copley always believed that proper artistic training was only available in Europe, and after 1774, when he left Boston and an increasingly tense political situation, he was able to work in London as a prominent court painter.

John Johnston, American, 1753–1818
Still Life, 1810
Oil on panel
14⅝ x 18⅛ in. (37.1 x 46.1 cm.)
Anonymous Gift 218:1966

John Johnston's *Still Life,* one of the
earliest American paintings of that genre,
depicts five ripe peaches, two clusters
of grapes, and a cut twig on a narrow
marbleized tabletop. Dew-like drops of
water appear on the table, leaves, and
fruit. A large bee is poised at the lower
left corner of the table, and a caterpillar
wiggles its way along one of the vines.
The ensemble is seen in sharp contrast to
the neutral white background, which is
as uninflected as the foreground elements
are modulated.

■

Charles F. Wimar, American, 1828–1862
The Captive Charger, 1854
Oil on canvas
30 x 41 in. (76.2 x 104.2 cm.)
Gift of Miss Lillie B. Randell 181:1925

Born in Germany, Wimar came to America with his family at the age of fifteen, settling in St. Louis. His stepfather ran a public house in the outskirts of the city near the area where Indians camped when they came to trade furs. The friendships young Charles made at the campground fostered a lifelong interest in native Americans.

After some local training in art, Wimar left St. Louis in 1851 to study at the Düsseldorf Art Academy and remained there until 1856. It was in Düsseldorf that Wimar conceived his life's goal of becoming a visual chronicler of the native American. In 1854, he painted *The Captive Charger,* a dramatic dusk scene of "…Indians returning from a foray,

having captured a Dragoon's horse." According to a contemporary traveler's report of a journey to the West, "All stealing is permissible among the Indians, but horse-stealing is honorable." Wimar gave the stolen horse's eyes an unsettled look which echoes the wariness of the men stealthily moving through the swamp.

Upon completing it, Wimar sent *The Captive Charger* to St. Louis, where it was sold in July of 1855 for $300. Wimar subsequently returned to St. Louis, where he was gaining recognition for his Indian scenes as well as portraits and genre scenes.

George Caleb Bingham, American,
1811–1879
Raftsmen Playing Cards, 1847
Oil on canvas
28 x 38 in. (71.2 x 96.5 cm.)
Purchase: Ezra H. Linley Fund 50:1934

In 1846, George Caleb Bingham sent a
group of four paintings to the American
Art-Union in New York. Included in the
set was *The Jolly Flatboatmen,* which was
purchased by the Art-Union, engraved,
and distributed to its membership across
the nation. The circulation of the print
marked the highest point Bingham's
career had reached thus far.

Bingham understood the implications
of the successful reception in New York
of paintings of Western life, and the
following year he submitted to the Art-
Union *Raftsmen Playing Cards,* which

builds upon the achievements of the
earlier picture. In this painting, the viewer
has moved onto the raft itself to observe
an early-morning card game. While one
raftsman, his back turned to the viewer,
poles the powerless craft downriver, the
carefully balanced central group passes
the time with cards. These boatmen,
though described as rowdy and unsavory
in eyewitness accounts, are depicted by
Bingham as civilized, genial, and passive.
To the viewer in the East, Bingham's
West appeared safe, secure, and happy,
with nature and man united.

■
George Caleb Bingham, American,
1811–1879
Jolly Flatboatmen in Port, 1857
Oil on canvas
47¹/₁₆ x 69⅝ in. (119.5 x 176.8 cm.)
Purchase 123:1944

When Bingham arrived in Europe for the
first time in 1856, he brought with him
the ambition of creating a history painting that would depict an important event
in the development of the American
West. He also brought along the memory
of his well-received paintings of river life
dating from the mid-1840s. These works,
which had given him national visibility,
suggested to him further potential.

After settling with his family in
Düsseldorf, Germany, Bingham set to
work on *Jolly Flatboatmen in Port*. With
more than nineteen figures, it was to be
his largest and most complex river paint-

ing. Moreover, unlike his earlier paintings of similar subjects, which were set in
remote bends of unnamed rivers, this
work was to depict a center of com-
merce, St. Louis. The scene shows a flatboat docked at the wharf, and boatmen
amusing themselves with their own
homespun entertainment, music, and
dancing. The revelry is so lively that
another flatboat has pulled alongside to
observe it. Bingham borrowed figures
from his earlier works for this painting;
the tour-de-force dancing figure who
holds a red handkerchief had appeared in
his best-known river painting, *Jolly Flatboatmen,* 1846.

John F. Kensett, American, 1816–1872
Upper Mississippi, 1855
Oil on canvas
18⅜ x 30¼ in. (46.7 x 76.9 cm.)
Purchase: Eliza McMillan Fund 22:1950

This Minnesota landscape of a site near
the headwaters of the Mississippi River
was painted during the period when
George Caleb Bingham was creating his
pictures of the Missouri and Mississippi
rivers. Although unruffled water is as
central to Kensett's view as it was to
Bingham's, the mountainous outcrop
plays a more dramatic role in Kensett's
work. On a sandy spit of land in the
painting's middle ground, Indians push

off their canoes into the smooth, blue-
gray water. Only the birds in the foreground, whose nests seem to be in the
rocky peaks at the left side of the canvas,
appear capable of breaking the spell of
calmness. Thinly painted and asymmetri-
cally structured, the "empty" scene utilizes
a format often employed by Kensett to
depict Lake George in the Adirondacks.
More than the landscape itself, it is the
presence of the Indians which places the
viewer in the West.

■

Winslow Homer, American, 1836–1910
The Country School, 1871
Oil on canvas
21⅜ x 38⅜ in. (54.3 x 97.5 cm.)
Purchase 123:1946

Winslow Homer developed his interest in scenes of everyday life as a magazine illustrator in the 1850s in Boston, where he worked primarily in the medium of wood engraving. His earliest paintings feature humble scenes rendered in contrasting lights and darks. Homer's images of American life show authentic characters in their native environments, without the overly sentimental qualities that mark many contemporary genre scenes.

In this painting, the artist depicts a rural schoolroom in an upstate New York town he had visited in 1870. The sunlight streaming through the window curtains suggests the fresh atmosphere of the country day and contrasts with the controlled geometry of the classroom. The horizontal organization of the students' benches leads into and across the compositional plane; the viewer's eyes, as the children's, focus on the teacher, whose solid triangular form is reinforced by the blackboard and the windows behind her. Homer further characterizes the classroom scene with spots of sunlight falling on desks and well-worn floorboards, as well as a captivating portrayal of the children's varying degrees of attention.

William M. Harnett, American,
1848–1892
With the Staats Zeitung, 1890
Oil on canvas
14⅛ x 20¼ in. (35.9 x 51.5 cm.)
Purchase 26:1945

Painted two years before the artist's death in 1892, William Harnett's *With the Staats Zeitung* looks back to his earlier compositions. The items on the wooden side table – the pewter-lidded stoneware tankard, the blue box of pipe tobacco, the folded German newspaper, the pipe, and five wooden matches – are symbols of masculine repose. While the newspaper appears unopened and unread, the pipe has been smoked recently; its ashes spill outward from its upside-down position.

Light enters from the left side of the composition, illuminating the metal rims on the pipe, the newspaper's deckle edge, and the highlighted joints of the tankard. The viewer seems to be in a quiet wood-paneled chamber. It is a room for simple, solitary indulgences such as drinking, smoking, and reading, activities which suggest the sensory pleasures of taste, sight, smell, and touch. The painting refers to the European tradition of depicting the senses, but does so with melancholic inwardness, rather than joyousness.

■

Thomas C. Eakins, American, 1844–1916
The Fairman Rogers Four-in-Hand,
1899
Oil on canvas
23½ x 35⅝ in. (59.7 x 90.6 cm.)
Purchase 92:1954

Like many nineteenth-century painters, Philadelphian Thomas Eakins frequently used photographs to aid him in creating his compositions. Eakins, who was also a photographer, was keenly interested in realistic representation.

The Fairman Rogers Four-in-Hand is a later *grisaille* version of an 1879 painting commissioned by Fairman Rogers and now owned by the Philadelphia Museum of Art. It depicts Rogers, with his wife and family members, driving his coach in Philadelphia's Fairmount Park. Rogers, one of the first people in the city to own and operate a four-in-hand coach, was an authority on coaching and published a manual on the subject in 1900. This later version of Eakins's 1879 painting was reproduced as the frontispiece for the manual.

Rogers was an amateur photographer who shared Eakins's interest in animal movement and how the camera could reveal its nuances. Both men studied the British photographer Eadweard Muybridge's images of horses in motion, which showed accurately the positions of the animals' legs in a gallop, canter, and trot. Eakins's 1879 rendering of the Rogers horses in fact is based upon his understanding of Muybridge's work, and the painting may be one of the first to represent the animals' movement realistically.

Augustus Saint-Gaudens, American,
1848–1907
Amor Caritas, 1898
Gilt bronze
39¾ x 17¼ in. (101.9 x 44.2 cm.)
Purchase 54:1927

Augustus Saint-Gaudens was born in
Dublin but came to America at the age
of six weeks. His early art training was in
New York City as a cameo cutter, and
during his educaton in Paris at the Ecole
des Beaux-Arts and later in Rome as a
sculptor, Saint-Gaudens used his cameo-
cutting skills to earn a living.

By the late 1870s, Saint-Gaudens had
begun to make a name for himself as a
talented sculptor of portraits as well as
historical and mythical figures in the
round or as bas-relief. A bas-relief, unlike
a free-standing sculpture, is carved out of
and engaged to a background, rather like
a large cameo.

Saint-Gaudens's Angel with Tablet, is
known as *Amor Caritas*. Originally created of clay in a high level of relief, this gilt
bronze piece is one of more than a dozen
copies cast from a less-than-half-sized
reduction of the original. The words
"Amor Caritas" on the tablet are Latin
for love and charity. The figure's face was
modeled from that of Saint-Gaudens's
mistress, Davida Clark. She wears a girdle and a crown of passion flowers.

One of the early casts of *Amor Caritas*
was purchased by the French government
and is now in the collection of the Louvre.
Saint-Gaudens was awarded the grand
prize in sculpture for this work at the
French Expositon Universelle of 1900.

Bessie Potter Vonnoh, American,
1872–1955
The Young Mother, 1896
Bronze
Height: 14½ in. (36.8 cm.)
Purchase: Given in memory of Henry
B. Pflager from his friends and wife,
Katherine King Pflager, by exchange
134:1985

By the time she was fourteen, St. Louis
native Bessie Vonnoh had decided she
wanted to be a sculptor. She later studied
with the famous American sculptor
Lorado Taft at the School of The Art
Institute of Chicago. For the World's
Columbian Exposition of 1893 in Chicago, Vonnoh created an eight-foot-high
allegorical figure of art for the Illinois
Building; she also worked on some of
Taft's pieces.

At the 1893 Exposition, Vonnoh
saw the small bronze figurines exhibited
by the Italian sculptor Prince Paul
Troubetskoy. Captivated by these
sculptural sketches, she began "doing
Troubetskoys," as she termed her new
diversion, which often explored the
elemental relationship between mothers
and their children. *The Young Mother* was
exhibited regularly. It received a bronze
medal at the Paris Exposition in 1900,
and an honorable mention at the 1901
Pan-American Exposition in Buffalo.

■

Thomas Wilmer Dewing, American,
1851–1938
Lady in White, c.1901
Oil on panel
20 x 15¾ in. (50.8 x 40 cm.)
Purchase: Museum Purchase, by
exchange; Museum Purchase and the
Eliza McMillan Purchase Fund 102:1988

Although not a familiar name today, in
the 1890s Thomas Wilmer Dewing was a
well-known and highly respected artist.
Born in Boston and apprenticed as a
young man to a lithographer, Dewing
finished his artistic education in Paris, as
was common for his generation, at the
Académie Julian.

By the late 1870s Dewing had settled
in New York City, and soon was recognized for his individualistic style. Before
long, Dewing's paintings, pastels, and
silverpoints were being collected by a
famous Detroit patron of the arts,
Charles Lang Freer. Freer was known for

his Asian collections as well as his habit
of acquiring the work of American artists
whom he felt emulated the Oriental
spirit in their work. One of Freer's part-
ners in this merger was St. Louisan
William K. Bixby, who had long been an
art collector. Through Freer, Bixby began
to buy Oriental art as well as the work of
American artists such as Dewing. *Lady in
White* was once part of Bixby's household
collection. Dewing painted many images
of this subject throughout his lifetime,
typically using a model to evoke a
dreamy, ageless figure in an undefined
space.

■

Maurice Prendergast, American,
1858–1924
Seashore, c.1910
Oil on canvas
24 x 32 in. (60.9 x 81.3 cm.)
Purchase: Eliza McMillan Fund 33:1948

Prendergast's paintings amalgamate a
number of advanced European artistic
movements from the end of the nineteenth century and the beginning of the
twentieth, resulting in a style which
nevertheless seems rooted in what one
must call "an American perspective."
Prendergast blended Impressionist subjects, Fauve color, and pointillist application of paint to create a distinctive style.

The elements of *Seashore* are defined
by its rich crust of paint. The purple sky,
shimmering blue-green water, and pink,
orange, green, and white dresses on the
silhouetted foreground figures create a

patterned decorative ensemble which
seems advanced yet Victorian, abstract yet
thoroughly representational. Prendergast's
feeling for abstraction is underscored by
the three bands of sky, water, and beach
that provide the basic structure of the
painting, and by the faceless figures of
the women who create a frieze-like band
in the foreground.

The mood of crowded anonymity
derives from Georges Seurat's *A Sunday
Afternoon on the Island of La Grande Jatte*
(The Art Institute of Chicago). The sense
of isolation is perhaps most aptly symbolized by the white sailboat bobbing in
solitary splendor just above the center of
the composition.

John Henry Twachtman, American,
1853–1902
The Rainbow's Source, c.1890–1900
Oil on canvas
34½ x 24½ in. (87.6 x 62.2 cm.)
Purchase 124:1921

This painting is one in a series of landscapes which depict Horseneck Falls on
the artist's farm in Greenwich, Connecti-
cut. Like their French counterparts,
American Impressionists such as Twachtman, Childe Hassam, and J. Alden Weir
often painted the same landscape motif
under different seasonal or atmospheric
conditions. In this painting, the falls are
presented almost head on, cascading into
a stream bed that winds its way to the
bottom of the canvas. The flat pictorial
space allows the falls, trees, and rocks to
coalesce into a carefully designed, almost
abstract, composition. The painting's
heavy underpainting, dry impasto, and
rough texture are all characteristic of
Twachtman's Greenwich period, when
his style was closest to Impressionism.

Frederick Carl Frieseke, American,
1874–1939
Torn Lingerie, 1915
Oil on canvas
51¼ x 51¾ in. (130.1 x 131.4 cm.)
Purchase 310:1916

An expatriate painter, Frieseke lived in
France for over forty years. After 1900,
when Frieseke began to spend his sum-
mers in Giverny, his work began to show
the influence of Impressionism. It was
probably Renoir, the Impressionist he
most admired, who most influenced
Frieseke in his focus on the intimate
subject of a woman in her boudoir for so
many paintings.

Frieseke was a virtuoso in capturing
the delicate frothiness of feminine finery.
In chalky shades of blue and pink, his
feathery brushstrokes surround the woman's figure with flowered wallpaper,
striped upholstery, and patterned rug.
The brightly colored blooms in the fresh
bouquet on the dressing table add
a vibrant note of color to an otherwise
pastel palette.

Paul Manship, American, 1885–1966
Centaur and Dryad, 1913
Bronze casting
Height: 29½ in. (74.9 cm.)
Purchase 74:1915

Paul Manship's diverse artistic education included the St. Paul Institute School of Art in Minnesota and the New York Art Students League. In 1909, Manship went to Rome on a three-year scholarship to the American Academy, where he was greatly influenced by classical art.

Soon after returning to the United States in 1912, Manship held a successful exhibition of his Roman work at the New York Architectural League. One of the most widely admired sculptures in the show was the *Centaur and Dryad.* Manship had begun the piece during his final year at the American Academy and

probably completed it in New York. The sculpture subsequently won the Helen Foster Barnett prize at the National Academy of Design.

In Greek mythology, the centaur belonged to a race of half-man, half-horse creatures. Homer described centaurs as wild beasts that were considered brutal, drunken, and lecherous. Dryads were wood nymphs. Around the base of Manship's rendition of a centaur pursuing a protesting dryad is a low relief of satyrs chasing meanads. Meanads and the half-man, half-goat satyrs comprised the retinue of Bacchus, the god of wine.

■

Robert Henri, American, 1865–1929
Betalo Rubino, Dramatic Dancer, 1916
Oil on canvas
77 x 37 in. (195.7 x 94 cm.)
Purchase 841:1920

Betalo Rubino was a well-known dancer
in New York. In Robert Henri's striking
full-length portrait, her black hair is
silhouetted by the freely brushed on
lime-green paint. The artist's virtuoso
brushwork is displayed in her deep-pink
lips, the richly impastoed orange of her
halter top and belt, the long black skirt
with four orange horizontal stripes, and
the red stockings and matching red
shoes. Within the dark skirt, Henri has
brushed on the black thickly at the edges
and thinly at the center, with thin grays
to suggest highlights. The dancer's face is
schematized in Henri's preferred manner.

A robust subject, powerfully executed,
Betalo Rubino might be a lower-class
descendant of one of John Singer
Sargent's wealthy patrons. While she
might remind the viewer of Sargent's *El
Jaleo* (Isabella Stewart Gardner Museum,
Boston), her earthiness, in combination
with Henri's daring and dramatic brushwork, bespeaks the inventiveness of "The
Eight," a group of American artists who
sought to depict urban and often lower-
class subjects in a freely painted manner.

John Storrs, American, 1885–1956
Modern Madonna, c.1918–1919
Terra-cotta, traces of paint
Height: 23⅜ in. (59.5 cm.)
Purchase: Museum Shop Fund 86:1985

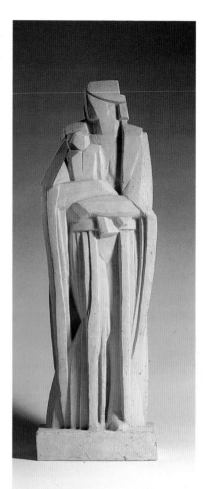

John Storrs's *Modern Madonna,* one of
the few terra-cotta sculptures known to
have been made by an American artist, is
also one of the rare American sculptures
that could be considered "Cubist." Nevertheless, the lovely salmon-colored wash
which tints its baked clay surface looks
back to eighteenth-century French masters of terra-cotta such as Clodion.

The stimulus for this piece appears to
have been the birth of Storrs's only child,
a daughter, in 1918. At that time, Storrs, a
Chicago-born artist who spent much of
his professional life in France, reworked
one of his designs for a medal honoring
French widows and orphans into a free-
standing sculpture. The artist's intention
was to render a traditional subject using
the most advanced and sculpturally chal-
lenging stylistic idioms of the day: Cubism and Art Deco. The cubistic elements
of the piece are the vertical slats of clay
that, like a pleated skirt, fall from the
Madonna's waist, and the angular reduction of the mother's arms and the child's
head, but the Cubist overlay seems
less convincing than the repetitive,
rhythmic forms of Art Deco. The figure's
skyscraper-like modernism appears to
transform a symbol of the European
tradition into an American office tower,
revealing the artist's roots on both sides
of the Atlantic.

■

Georgia O'Keeffe, American, 1887–1986
Birch Trees at Dawn on Lake George,
1926
Oil on canvas
36 x 30 in. (91.4 x 76.2 cm.)
Gift of Mrs. Ernest W. Stix 14:1964

Georgia O'Keeffe was one of several American artists who introduced the principles of modern European abstract art in the United States in the early part of this century. Though she lived and worked for a time in New York City – largely because of her association with the photographer and gallery owner Alfred Stieglitz – O'Keeffe was always drawn to open country, particularly to the American Southwest. She developed a personal language of semi-abstract forms and used it to suggest the imagery and moods of nature.

In this painting, the curvaceous, tubular shapes and light colors evoke breeze-struck birch trees arching in the early morning light, but they also appear sensuous and even torso-like in their organicism. In fact, this organicism recalls Stieglitz's probing, often abstract photographs of O'Keeffe taken at Lake George, a site in upstate New York where the Stieglitz family kept a summer home, and where he and O'Keeffe often escaped from urban life.

■

Paul Manship, American, 1885–1966
Celestial Sphere, 1934
Bronze
Diameter: 20½ in. (52 cm.)
Gift: J. Lionberger Davis Trust 284:1955

Manship created this sphere as a guide to
the heavens. Arranged at the latitude of
forty degrees north, the globe has the
North Star at the top and a horizontal
band at the horizon line. A female figure
floating on a bed of clouds supports the
orb of stars above. Her dark supine figure
suggests the night that contains the sixty-
six constellations revealed in the evening

sky. Each of the bronze constellations is
punctuated with cast silver stars which
represent the actual position and intensity of the stars that define the constellations for us.

More than an accurate representation
of how we see the heavens, this sculpture
of the zodiac reveals Manship's interest in
the heritage of mythology. For Manship,
the constellations signified the connec-
tions between modern man and his ancient past.

Thomas Hart Benton, American,
1889–1975
Cradling Wheat, 1938
Tempera and oil on board
31 x 38 in. (78.7 x 96.5 cm.)
Purchase 8:1939

Thomas Hart Benton, a native of Kansas City, Missouri, was one of a group of artists working in the 1930s known as the Regionalists. Influenced by the Populist politics and nationalist sentiments of the time, Benton, like the painters Grant Wood and John Steuart Curry, was intent on capturing in his art the images of grassroots America which were rapidly disappearing in the face of developing industrialization. In fact, Benton spurned both urban cosmopolitanism and ensuing American Modernist trends to focus on painting homespun subject matters in a descriptive style. Scenes of rural laborers and the urban working class are common in his art. He often deflected the faces of his figures, as in this painting, or generalized them to suggest their universal qualities. This work exemplifies Benton's use of strongly contrasting colors and boldly drawn forms, which move in a circular fashion throughout the composition and enliven a typical scene of humble field workers on a Midwestern farm.

Modern Art

■

Claude Monet, French, 1840–1926
**The Promenade with the Railroad
Bridge, Argenteuil,** 1874
Oil on canvas
21½ x 28¾ in. (54.8 x 73 cm.)
Gift of Sydney M. Shoenberg, Sr. 45:1973

In 1874, Claude Monet was living in
Argenteuil, a village on the Seine just a
short train ride north from the center of
Paris. To depict the suburb's mix of the
pastoral and the modern, Monet included the railroad bridge in his painting as a
central compositional element, using the
same hurried brushstrokes which distinguish the bucolic motifs of water and sky.
Several months after this picture was
finished, the Impressionist painters
staged the first of their now famous eight
exhibitions in Paris. The group's free
brushstrokes and elimination of traditional shading, which now seem to evoke

the breezes of a spring day, were considered at the time a travesty of the established conventions of painting. Moreover,
the selection of urban and suburban
themes was viewed as vulgar in the
extreme.

Now we see the admittedly loose
structure of this painting as being held
together by Monet's adoption of the
compositional principles of Japanese
printmaking. The fact that the woman
with the parasol and her child, Monet's
wife Camille and their son Jean, do not
relate to a defined narrative context, and
that their faces are not finely shaded,
suggests the momentary way one views
figures walking randomly through a
landscape. The paint is, in places, very
thinly applied; the base canvas shows
both in the water and in the sky.

Edgar Degas, French, 1834–1917
Little Dancer of Fourteen Years,
c.1880–1881
Bronze
Height: 38½ in. (97.6 cm.)
Gift of Mrs. Mark C. Steinberg 135:1956

The powerful attraction the performing arts exercised on Degas complemented his efforts to chronicle aspects of contemporary Parisian life. In addition to depicting ballet performances, he eventually gained admission to the rehearsal rooms, where he observed and drew the so-called "rats," the girls who made up the ballet chorus. These young women were not stars but the underlings upon which the ballet ran, and Degas found their anonymity appealing.

Little Dancer of Fourteen Years, based on Degas's studies of a young Belgian girl, has startlingly life-like features. The little dancer's pose hovers between the suppleness of childhood and the self-awareness of a young woman. Degas included the wax model of the sculpture in the Impressionist exhibition of 1881, adding a wig of human hair, a satin bow, an actual though miniaturized tutu, ballet slippers, and wooden flooring as a base.

Little Dancer was the only sculpture Degas exhibited during his lifetime. As with the rest of his sculptural oeuvre, the wax models were cast by his estate after the artist died. The St. Louis piece is one of approximately twenty-three bronze casts after the wax original. The sculptures were "dressed" to resemble the presentation of the wax model, with bronze simulacra of the original hair, bodice, and shoes.

■

Paul Cézanne, French, 1839–1906
The Bathers, 1890–1892
Oil on canvas
20¾ x 25¼ in. (52.7 x 64.2 cm.)
Gift of Mrs. Mark C. Steinberg 2:1956

From his youth in southern France,
Paul Cézanne derived an arcadian view
of women as leading simple, quiet lives.
He went on to paint pictures of women
bathing in modern settings for much of
his career, but these works reached a cre-
scendo of maturity and intensity during
the last six years of his life. The largest of
the late paintings have various unfinished
aspects, and yet each is a sumptuous and
complete work of art. The series appears
to be the final major statement of this
most cautious of painters.

The St. Louis painting originally was
owned by a fellow Impressionist and a
member of Cézanne's own generation,
Claude Monet. One can speculate about
the influence that Cézanne's canvas
might have had upon Monet during his
late period, as both artists moved beyond
their Impressionist modes to more per-
sonalized styles.

Although most of Cézanne's bathers
are women, the St. Louis work is composed largely of male subjects. The
painting has a sense of completeness, a
finished quality which many subsequent
versions lack. The blue sky that domi-
nates the canvas is prominent in all of
Cézanne's late works. It often evokes a
troubled feeling, with the bathers posing
among the foreground trees in a frieze-
like arrangement. Here, however, the
mood is more reposeful, less anxious. It is
one of the most complete and tranquil
late works by the father of modern art.

■

Vincent van Gogh, Dutch, 1853–1890
Stairway at Auvers, 1890
Oil on canvas
20 x 28 in. (50.8 x 71.1 cm.)
Purchase 1:1935

After a breakdown and convalescence in an asylum in Arles, in the south of France, Vincent van Gogh spent the last period of his life in the village of Auvers, northwest of Paris. Despite his ill health, he was extremely prolific at this time, inspired by his new surroundings. "Auvers is quite beautiful," the artist wrote to his brother Theo in Paris, "many thatched roofs, among others, something that is becoming rather scarce… It is of a grave beauty, the real countryside, characteristic and picturesque."

The two van Gogh paintings from this period in the Museum's collection were completed within weeks of one another in late May and early June of 1890. In this particular work the artist depicts a street scene in Auvers, with the path and stairway rendered in converging, snake-like forms. These dynamic rhythms are not so much a result of the artist's troubled mental state as an interpretation of the townscape's undulating walls and changes in street levels. The figures also are treated as sinuous forms, and so are unified with the town itself. Van Gogh's use of vivid, intense color and visible, highly texturized brushstrokes heightens and enlivens a simple rural scene, and opens the door to the expressionist tendencies in twentieth-century painting.

Paul Gauguin, French, 1848–1903
Portrait of Madame Roulin, 1888
Oil on canvas
19¼ x 24½ in. (48.8 x 62.2 cm.)
Gift of Mrs. Mark C. Steinberg 5:1959

In the fall of 1888, Paul Gauguin visited his friend Vincent van Gogh in Arles, in the south of France. The atmosphere of his stay was tense, since the artists' admiration for each other's work was offset by their strong personalities and frequent disagreements. "Vincent and I hardly see eye to eye, especially in regard to painting," Gauguin stated.

The painters' differences are exemplified by their artistic treatment of Madame Roulin, the matriarch of an Arles family to whom both were drawn as a portrait subject. In van Gogh's painting, now at the Museum of Fine Arts in Boston, heavy brushwork and jagged lines make for an agitated, dynamic portrayal of the sitter. By contrast, Gauguin emphasizes her stability and calm; her massive form fills the canvas from top to bottom, weighing heavily on the right half of the composition, and her placid expression is firm amid the painting's vivid and starkly contrasting colors. The canvas Gauguin represents in the background is one of his own, *Landscape with Blue Trees,* 1888, and adds to the decorative surface arrangement of the painting.

In works he completed during his visit to Arles, Gauguin continued to explore the methods of "Cloisonism," a manner of painting upon which he had focused with a group of artists earlier that summer in Brittany. The outlined segments of bold, flat color in this canvas recall the broad areas of color common to stained glass and medieval cloisonné enamels.

Georges Seurat, French, 1859–1891
**Port-en-Bessin: The Outer Harbor,
Low Tide,** 1888
Oil on canvas
21⅛ x 25⅞ in. (53.6 x 65.7 cm.)
Purchase 4:1934

Nineteenth-century color theories influenced painters of the period in different ways. Delacroix's technique, for example, made bright, contrasting colors blend in the viewer's eye, and the Impressionists used color and brushwork to suggest the effects of light on the dissolution of forms seen in nature. Seurat's approach, on the other hand, was rigid and almost scientific. His characteristic painting method, which he called "Divisionism"

and which has since become known as Pointillism or Neo-Impressionism, involved the construction of a composition by means of a complex system of regularly applied and variously shaped small dabs of color. He limited his palette to the colors of the spectrum, for he felt that in this way forms could be suggested as they appeared in atmospheric light.

Seurat spent the summer of 1888 in Port-en-Bessin on the Normandy coast of France, and produced five paintings of the harbor. The geometric structure of the scene – the vertical and horizontal forms of the docks, the water line, and the horizon – attracted the artist as an appropriate composition to depict the structure of color. Such formal stability lends a sense of calm to the quiet marine vista.

Claude Monet, French, 1840–1926
Water Lilies, c. 1919–1926
Oil on canvas
78¾ x 167¾ in. (200 x 426 cm.)
Gift of the Steinberg Charitable Fund
134:1956

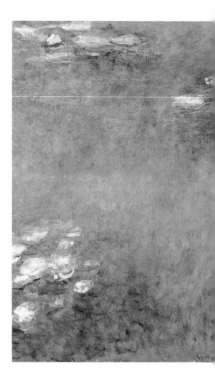

At the time of the 1978 exhibition
Monet's Years at Giverny, it was discovered
that three large paintings by the artist
were not individual canvases but parts of
a single enormous triptych. The three
panels, owned by The Nelson-Atkins
Museum of Art, the Cleveland Museum
of Art, and The Saint Louis Art Museum,
were reunited in that exhibition. As they
can function both individually and collec-
tively, the panels are a testament to the
breadth of Monet's late works.

The St. Louis painting, the triptych's
central element, strikes the final chord in
Monet's rich evolution as an artist. Executed half a century after *The Promenade
with the Railroad Bridge, Argenteuil* (p.
184), the panel represents a natural transformation of Monet's initial vision. Although water is the tacit subject of both
works, in the earlier painting water, air,
and other natural forms retain their dis-
crete functions and characters, while in
the later canvas, all "landscape" elements
converge into a whole. Gone are the river
banks, the strolling mother and child,
the railroad bridge. Instead, the artist
subsumes himself within the gentle
rhythms and shapes of water and aquatic
life. The structure of the painting is rooted
in expanding and gently nuanced rays of
color, locked into place by clusters of
loosely shaped floating lily pads.

■
Wassily Kandinsky, Russian, 1866–1944
Winter Landscape, 1911
Oil on canvas
37⅝ x 41⅛ in. (95.6 x 104.5 cm.)
Bequest of Morton D. May 142:1986

Winter Landscape is among the most
radically simplified compositions of
Kandinsky's years in Murnau, a very
productive period during which he
painted pictures that teetered on the
brink of almost complete abstraction.
The subject is simply a locomotive passing through a valley coated in snow.
The dominant element in the painting
is the snow-covered tree in the right
foreground. Its umbrella-like form, painted in thin washes of blue, pink, and
white, acts as a *repoussoir* element which
defines the foreground and against which
the other elements recede. The locomotive hurtles along behind the tree and
along child-like tracks, brownish smoke
belching from its metal stack. In the near
distance are pyramidal snow-covered
hills, and further back are the barren
brown caps of mountains.

Kandinsky devised the most econom-
ical pictorial means to probe the farthest
reaches of what can constitute a complete
work of art; he was among the first artists
of the twentieth century to both investi-
gate this question and provide a powerful
answer. His distillation of narrow artistic
means proved so rich in implication and
meaning that the twin threads of abstraction and representation being explored
by contemporary artists find their headwaters in such paintings as Kandinsky's
Winter Landscape.

Lyonel Feininger, American, 1871–1956
Woman with Green Eyes, 1915
Oil on canvas
27½ x 24 in. (70 x 61 cm.)
Bequest of Morton D. May 887:1983

Lyonel Feininger is best known for his successful blending of the Modernist style with Romantic subjects such as gothic townscapes and seascapes with tall sailing ships. Feininger was born in New York City. His parents, both successful musicians, took him to Germany at the age of sixteen to attend the Leipzig Conservatory. However, Feininger studied drawing and painting instead. He later settled in Berlin, supporting himself with earnings from caricatures and illustrations. These were at first quite conventional, but soon began to take on the rough-hewn distortions that gained him an international reputation. A 1906 contract from *The Chicago Sunday Tribune*

for the comic strips "Kin-der Kids" and "Wee Willie Winkie's World" allowed Feininger to move to Paris for two years. There he found the creative freedom and artistic contacts that enabled him to abandon cartooning and commit himself to painting.

Woman with Green Eyes was inspired by the features of Feininger's second wife, Julia, and harkens back to his early caricature portraits. Unlike his landscape views, this rare figure study is assertively flat. The large areas of color and lack of spatial intricacies call to mind the Fauvist portraits of Matisse. However, Feininger's refined and conservative sense of color softens the image, creating a harmonious surface.

Ludwig Meidner, German, 1884–1966
Burning City, 1913
Oil on canvas
26½ x 31¼ in. (68.5 x 80.5 cm.)
Bequest of Morton D. May 913:1983

Ludwig Meidner was born in Bernstadt, Silesia, where his parents ran a textile business. In 1906, after studying painting at the Breslau art school and working briefly in Berlin as a fashion artist, his interest in French Impressionism took him to Paris, where he studied the works of Manet and Cézanne and became a friend of Amedeo Modigliani.

After returning to Berlin in 1908, Meidner executed a series of paintings, drawings, and prints based on the city. These works, completed in 1912–1913, established his early reputation as "the most expressionistic of the Expression-

ists." Meidner found inspiration for his city views in the texts of the Italian Futurists and in French painter Robert Delaunay's fractured views of the Eiffel Tower. In 1913, the year he painted *Burning City,* Meidner wrote: "A street is composed not of tonal values but is a bombardment of whizzing rows of windows, of rushing beams of light between vehicles of many kinds, of a thousand leaping spheres, tatters of people, billboards, and droning shapeless masses of color." *Burning City* is a compelling image that prefigures the devastation of World War I. The ground heaves and collapses, sucking the buildings and their inhabitants down into a vortex of destruction. Meidner's post-War paintings lost this violent expressionism; the artist became deeply involved with religion and poetry, leaving behind the apocalyptic visions of his early work.

Ernst Ludwig Kirchner, German,
1880–1938
Circus Rider, 1914
Oil on canvas
80 x 59¼ in. (202 x 150.5 cm.)
Bequest of Morton D. May 904:1983

Many of the innovations of the French Impressionist painters and their successors were warmly received and adapted by progressive German painters of the early twentieth century. In his interior views of cafe life or his exterior scenes of desolate urban sites, Kirchner drew upon subjects first broached by Edgar Degas and Henri Toulouse-Lautrec, and later by Claude Monet and Pierre-Auguste Renoir. The use of intensive, dissonant color derives from a subsequent generation of French artists, the Fauve painters, who in the period near 1905 pried color loose from its representational functions.

Early twentieth-century German painters not only studied French models but used these resources to release their own powerful and imaginative tools. In *Circus Rider,* a vibrant clashing vortex of color and form is created by the overlay of the circus ring's dark-red concentric circles with inset green and yellow circles that suggest footlights. Cutting across this tapestry is the silhouetted black form of the circus horse and rider; above it is the peculiar form of the clown, and below are the ringmaster and members of the audience. Like Max Beckmann, Kirchner was drawn to the circus as a rich source of inspiration; but whereas Beckmann's use of the circus motif retains a narrative element, the theme takes on the air of the fantastic with Kirchner.

Max Beckmann, German, 1884–1950
The Sinking of the Titanic, 1912–1913
Oil on canvas
104⅜ x 130 in. (265 x 330 cm.)
Bequest of Morton D. May 840:1983

Just as news reports of the rescue of a
nautical disaster inspired Théodore
Géricault in the 1830s to create a heroic
contemporary history painting, *The Raft
of the Medusa,* so did the tragic sinking
of the ocean liner *Titanic* in 1912 inspire
the young Max Beckmann. By that time,
Beckmann had already executed a number of works with Biblical and matholog-
ical themes, in a youthful attempt to
breathe fresh life into history painting of
the period. In this quest, Beckmann
looked to French prototypes to create a
dignified figural vocabulary. *The Sinking
of the Titanic* conflates Géricault's *Raft*

with Delacroix's *Barge of Dante,* combin-
ing both French Romantic giants in a
single modern visual premise.

The young Beckmann's ambition is
reflected in the sensational subject and
the enormous size of the canvas. He
mythologizes the event, and the disas-
trous situation seems a prescient symbol
of the perilous state of Europe on the
brink of World War I. Incorporated into
the structure of the painting are innovations in the use of color linked to both
German Expressionism and Fauvism.
Greens and rich purples appear on the
victims' faces, yet the colors are not completely integrated into the fabric of the
painting itself.

For all its ambition, the *Titanic* is a
youthful expression, lacking the enormous economy of brushwork and format
that characterized Beckmann's mature
work. Even so, the painting reveals the
deep passions that underlie later, more
modestly sized canvases.

Max Beckmann, German, 1884–1950
The Dream, 1921
Oil on canvas
71⅝ x 35¼ in. (182 x 91 cm.)
Bequest of Morton D. May 841:1983

As in a dream, the vertical jumble of six
figures in Beckmann's painting is filled
with deeper meaning and significance
than is initially apparent. The narrative is
situated within an artist's garret, and we
see empty picture frames on the far wall
and lower left foreground. The upper-
most figure, who has bandaged stumps
instead of hands, stands on a ladder
holding a fish. To his left, a blind beggar
blows a horn while playing his sad hand
organ. Beneath these two male figures,
an innocent blond-haired woman sits
with her palm expressively open, holding
a Pulcinello doll. She is the only figure
whose eyes are open. Facing her is a pris-
oner on crutches with stumps for legs,
and in the foreground, a drunken woman plays a stringless and damaged violin.

What is the viewer to make of this
assemblage? The painting has the feel of
an ancient parable on the folly of human
existence. The figures' demeanor recalls
Gothic saints, and the props they hold –
fish, organ, violin, Pulcinello – become
timeless attributes which accompany
humankind through the darkness.

On a personal level, *The Dream* reflects Beckmann's observation and deeply
felt experience of the carnage of World
War I. The painting, one of the finest
from Beckmann's Frankfurt period, symbolizes the troubled state of post-War
Germany and presents a tragic view of
twentieth-century man which, despite
technological progress, harks back to the
attitudes of the Middle Ages.

Max Beckmann, German, 1884–1950
Acrobats, 1939
Oil on canvas
Left: 78½ x 35½ in. (200 x 90 cm.)
Center: 78½ x 67 in. (200 x 170 cm.)
Right: 78½ x 35½ in. (200 x 90 cm.)
Bequest of Morton D. May 851:1983

More than a dozen figures bind together the panels of this triptych. In the central panel, a woman with a crown holds a globe. A blond-haired woman in a white skirt looks away from her and towards the snake tamer in blue tights, who has a snake wrapped around his body. A tiny midget with a drum runs between the two female figures.

In the left panel, the viewer looks down from the top of the circus. A dramatically foreshortened acrobat swings across the upper section. Beneath him on the tightrope is an embracing couple, and further below on the safety net, a woman in a polka-dotted dress holds a bird. A waiter in black tie brings champagne to the couple. In the far right-hand scene, a seated ice cream vendor, her form framed by the edge of the mirror behind her, talks to a man in a Roman centurion costume. In the foreground, two masked dwarfs perched atop a table drink champagne.

In this painting, as in *The Dream* of 1921, Beckmann uses circus images which speak on a metaphorical level to the past and the present. While *The Dream* characterizes the traumatic effect of World War I, *Acrobats* defines the balancing act of forces in pre-World War II Europe. The circus costumes, activities, and intensive interior setting allow Beckmann to spell out his dark view of human nature and the world. The work's title refers not only to the theme of circus performers, but also to what Beckmann saw as the role of the artist and his art: taking risks, thrilling the viewer, and astonishing the mind and the senses.

Max Beckmann, German, 1884–1950
Self-Portrait in Blue Jacket, 1950
Oil on canvas
55⅛ x 36 in. (140 x 91 cm.)
Bequest of Morton D. May 866:1983

In 1949, Max Beckmann left St. Louis, where he had taught painting at Washington University since 1947, for New York City. The following year, the artist painted his last self-portrait, *Self-Portrait in Blue Jacket.*

As in his well-known *Self-Portrait in Tuxedo* of 1927, Beckmann is seen directly and at three-quarter length, with the rich hue of his jacket creating the defining color note of the painting. The cigarette Beckmann holds to his lips plays an important role, as does the placement of one hand in a pocket.

Both paintings appear direct yet withhold themselves, just as Beckmann's formal bearing and attire distance him from the viewer. The artist, who in pose seems to want to reveal himself so directly, looks askance, beyond the viewer, avoiding contact.

This painting is the end of a sequence which began with Beckmann's earliest self-portrait, *Self-Portrait in Florence,* 1907, and ran steadily throughout the artist's career. The series of self-portraits has been compared to Rembrandt's, but is far cooler in sensibility than that of the great seventeenth-century Dutch master. As the final painting in the sequence, this work underscores Beckmann's achievement of defining the validity of the portrait for post–World War II Europe and America.

Henri Matisse, French, 1869–1954
Bathers with a Turtle, 1908
Oil on canvas
70½ x 86¾ in. (179.1 x 220.3 cm.)
Gift of Mr. and Mrs. Joseph Pulitzer, Jr.
24:1964

Pablo Picasso's *Les Desmoiselles d'Avignon,* executed in 1907, is widely regarded as one of the most important paintings of the twentieth century. The depiction of three female figures, two standing and one crouching, is a linchpin for the study of Cubism. Picasso's only rival for the leadership of French painting of the period, Henri Matisse, well may have seen *Les Desmoiselles* in the artist's studio, and he seems to have responded to it the following year in this painting of three female figures, *Bathers with a Turtle.*

A comparison of the two artists' treatment of the subject distinguishes two major directions for twentieth-century art. Matisse's painting is less confrontational and more ingratiating than Picasso's distorted physiognomies; albeit touched with anxiety, his view is more arcadian than Picasso's. One of Matisse's figures, turned away from the viewer, sits on her haunches to feed a turtle, an ancient symbol of eternity. The left-hand figure's activity is observed by the standing central figure and, possibly, by the withdrawn figure on the right who sits on the grass. Behind the women, the landscape consists of three single bands: grass, water, and sky. The bodies are executed in mottled, flesh colors, outlined with black and heightened by pink.

Matisse's world of lyrical shapes and expanses of nuanced color is fully expressed in *Bathers with a Turtle.* The work is a mature statement which draws upon the painter's earlier achievements and forecasts the direction of his artistic concerns from 1908 until his death in 1954.

Pablo Picasso, Spanish, 1881–1973
The Fireplace, 1916
Oil on canvas
58¾ x 27½ in. (149.2 x 69.9 cm.)
Gift of Joseph Pulitzer, Jr. 81:1970

Cubism, Pablo Picasso's radical new
method of painting, marked a watershed
in the history of twentieth-century art.
Picasso's treatment of largely traditional
subjects by suggesting their forms, vol-
umes, and surrounding space as inter-
secting geometric planes was an attempt
to reconcile three-dimensional illusion
to a two-dimensional canvas.

The fireplace is a subject Picasso
treated in this and two other paintings,
executed in 1915 and 1916: in the earlier
work he concentrated on a vibrant surface design and texture, while in the
second canvas he depicted a greater sense
of spatial depth. In this painting, Picasso
fused these two interests to represent the
spatial variances that coexist in the visible
world. The overlapping, multitextured
forms of the still-life group atop the
mantel, especially the curvaceous shape of
the guitar, make for a rich surface interest
distinct from the more flatly geometric
definition of the fireplace below. Depth is
portrayed by means of the diagonal line
that suggests the fireplace interior and,
simultaneously, by the reflection of the
still life in the mantel mirror.

Pablo Picasso, Spanish, 1881–1973
Pitcher and Fruit Bowl, 1931
Oil on canvas
51⅛ x 75⅞ in. (130 x 195 cm.)
Bequest of Morton D. May 932:1983

Picasso explored many subjects in refining his engagement with the Cubist compositional methods he had forged at the beginning of the twentieth century. He frequently used traditional art-historical subjects as vehicles for his highly innovative treatments. In the early 1930s, while living in the town of Boisgeloup outside Paris, he painted a series of large still lifes, executed with curving lines that intersect to both suggest the forms of the objects and fracture them, much like traditional Cubist compositions.

With this work, however, Picasso was less interested in precise analysis of forms in space than in creating a rythmic, decorative painting. Against the pale white and off-white of the background, the purple, green, and red areas, as well as the heavy black lines, evoke stained glass. The textured application of paint calls additional attention to the lively surface. Nevertheless, Picasso's overall treatment of the lush colors suggests the still life's sensuousness in a restrained fashion, as the vivid colors on one hand and the linearity of forms on the other create a compositional balance.

Amedeo Modigliani, Italian, 1884–1920
Elvira Resting at a Table, 1919
Oil on canvas
36⅜ x 23⅞ in. (93.3 x 61.2 cm.)
Gift of Joseph Pulitzer, Jr. in memory of
his wife, Louise Vauclain Pulitzer 77:1968

A child of the streets from the neighbor-
hood of Modigliani's Parisian studio was
the sitter for this painting. Following
principles of construction indebted to
Cézanne, Modigliani adjusted her form
and her position in space to his own
pictorial ends. The viewer approaches the
figure directly, yet sees the wooden table
next to her from above; this arrangement
compresses the sitter, cutting her off
from the viewer.

The girl's blank eye sockets and mask-
like face neutralize the more specific
aspects of her appearance, personality,
and location, as if she were both a particular person and a generic type. As a
"type," she represents a conflation of
African and Iberian sculpture and the
stylized facial forms of Byzantine mosa-
ics. Thus, the waif evokes the rich past of
Western and African cultures as the artist
underscores the true pathos of the situation: the frail girl whose future is probably not very bright is seen as a vessel for
the beauty of the past.

Alberto Giacometti, Swiss, 1901–1966
Hands Holding the Void, 1934–1935
Bronze
Height: 60¾ in. (154.5 cm.)
Purchase: Friends Fund 217:1966

This spindly figure stares out in per-
petual wide-eyed amazement, its hand
reaching out, open fingered. A plinth
rests upon its feet. Though tacitly a female, the sculpture has an androgynous
presence.

The figure looks at the viewer, but
with the startled demeanor of someone
awakened in the middle of a dream. Such
was the ambition of Giacometti and
other artists of the Surrealist movement:
to create a visual equivalent for uncon-
scious experience. However, in evoking
the realm of dreams, Surrealist sculpture
usually depends more on juxtaposition
of unrelated objects than upon single
images such as this.

In *Hands Holding the Void,* Giacometti
was able to state a sense of sexual anxiety
and of dream imagery using the vocabulary of figural sculpture. This achievement is analogous to the Belgian painter
René Magritte's ability to evoke the
Surrealist enterprise by means of seemingly academic techniques. Giacometti
developed further than Magritte in this
respect, however, transposing expression
and eloquent poses into the rugose surfaces of his later sculptures. It is in works
such as *Hands Holding the Void* that the
existential quality of those pieces finds its
roots.

Philip Guston, American, 1913–1980
Martial Memory, 1941
Oil on canvas
40⅛ x 32¼ in. (101.9 x 81.9 cm.)
Purchase: Eliza McMillan Fund 115:1942

Philip Guston completed *Martial Memory* in New York City shortly before moving to the Midwest to begin teaching at the University of Iowa. This classically composed picture, which Guston considered his first mature oil painting, is infused with the mood of urban melancholy widespread among pre-World War II American artists like Ben Shahn. The piece reflects Guston's fondness for the balanced compositions of Italian Renaissance painters such as Piero della Francesca. It also testifies to the artist's admiration for the serious, even majestic, figural style of Max Beckmann, whose works Guston first saw in New York in the 1930s. Six years after this painting was completed, Guston began teaching at Washington University in St. Louis; when he left, his position was filled by Beckmann himself.

Martial Memory is a rich inventory of formal motifs which reappear in Guston's late work: hooded figures, garbage can lids, even the children's shoes. While the combat of the boys is descriptive in this painting, in the artist's late works the theme of warfare becomes internalized and more autobiographical, rather than narrative.

Philip Guston, American, 1913–1980
Room 112, 1957
Oil on canvas
62 x 68⅜ in. (157.5 x 173.5 cm.)
Gift of Mr. and Mrs. Joseph Pulitzer, Jr.
249:1966

In the late 1940s and early 1950s, Philip
Guston developed a personal style of
abstraction. His odd-shaped but richly
painted units of pink, blue, gray, green,
and black huddle together, as if attracted
to each other by a form of gravitational
force. With Willem De Kooning and
Franz Kline, Guston contributed to the
gestural current within the Abstract
Expressionist group.

The date of *Room 112,* 1957, marks
the high point in the development of
Guston's abstract style. By the end of the
decade, the lengthy process of his disen-
chantment with abstraction had begun.
He slowly drained the color out of his
abstract paintings, and then sought to
invent a personal figural imagery. It was
not until a dozen years after *Room 112*
was executed that the pictorial elements
of Guston's late style crystallized.

■
David Smith, American, 1906–1965
Cockfight, 1945
Steel
Height: 45 in. (114.5 cm.)
Purchase 188:1946

David Smith was born in Decatur,
Illinois, and studied at the Art Students
League in New York. After graduating
he became linked with the New York
School, which included the painters
Jackson Pollock and Willem De Kooning,
among others. In the early 1930s Smith
became intrigued by Picasso's welded
steel sculptures of 1928–1929, and began
to experiment with constructed sculpture.

Cockfight, which can be considered
a starting point for Smith's sculptural
ambitions, was among the first of his
pieces to enter the collection of an
American museum. The two silhouetted
forms of cocks locked in deadly combat
have been interpreted as an allegory of
the battles raging in Europe in 1945, or of
the aggressive ambitions of New York
School artists at the end of the Second
World War. The fundamental devices in
Cockfight – balanced stack forms, arc-
welded steel, silhouetted shapes framed
in space – are essential components of
Smith's subsequent works, and were
refined to their highest degree almost
twenty years later in his *Cubi* series.

Henry Moore, British, 1898–1986
Standing Figure, 1950
Bronze
Height: 86 in. (218.5 cm.)
Gift of Mr. and Mrs. Richard K. Weil
316:1980

In 1921, after two years at Leeds College
of Art, Henry Moore arrived in London
to continue his studies with a scholarship
from the Royal College of Art. While
in London he frequented the British
Museum, whose collections of Egyptian,
Etruscan, Mexican, Oceanic, and African
sculpture had a great impact on his early
pieces. In the 1930s Moore abandoned
the more overtly primitive characteristics
of his work to embrace the organic forms
he is perhaps best known for. When
Moore's London studio was bombed
during World War II, he moved to Much
Hadham, Hertfordshire, where he settled
permanently. Living in the country inspired Moore's sense of monumentality
as he began to see his sculptures surrounded only by hills and sky.

The human figure was always at the
core of Moore's work. *Standing Figure* is a
monumental example of his experiments
in opening the sculptural form and
reducing the supports needed to link
shapes. Interestingly, Moore spoke about
this piece as having been influenced by
the work of the Italian Baroque artist
Giovanni Bernini, who was not a personal favorite but whose control of materials, bold cutting away of supports, and
exquisitely contorted sculptural forms
Moore admired.

Joseph Cornell, American, 1903–1972
Isabelle (Dien Bien Phu), 1954
Box construction with glass, painted
wood, paper collage, and mirror
18 x 12 x 6 in. (45.8 x 30.5 x 15.3 cm.)
Purchase: Funds given by the Shoenberg
Foundation, Inc. 181:1986

Joseph Cornell spent his adult life
collecting the flotsam and jetsam of
civilization and using his finds to create
artistic collages in small, open-faced
wooden boxes. The collage construction
Isabelle is one of a long series about birds,
especially cockatoos. Cornell presents a
symbol of man, whose world has been
shattered and whose blood has been
spilled. The mounted cut-out of the
cockatoo sits behind a piece of shattered
glass. Around the bird, red paint is splat-
tered like blood on the white painted
interior.

The box is meant to be looked at
from both sides. On the lower-left back
corner, a collaged portion of a newspaper
article reads:

*A hard core band of 2,000 Foreign Legion-
naires chose to go down fighting for the
glory of France in a suicidal attack on the
Communist captors of Dien Bien Phu. The
High French Command at Hanoi said the
Legionnaires under the command of Col.
André La Lande at outpost "Isabelle" preferred to fight to the end than to surrender.
A communist* [sic] *Radio Peking broadcast
heard in Tokyo said the Communist In-
dochinese conquerors of Dien Bien Phu
"annihilated" the Legionnaires hours after
the main fortress had fallen.*

The 1950s were an insular, self-
involved period for Americans. It would
seem that Cornell assembled this image
with the intention of reminding his
country that it is not an island. Cornell's
works are oftentimes not merely clever
constructs, but obtuse social and political
statements assembled from the remnants
of our time and culture.

■
Mark Rothko, American, 1903–1970
Red, Orange, Orange on Red, 1962
Oil on canvas
92 x 80½ in. (233.7 x 204.5 cm.)
Purchase: Funds given by the Shoenberg
Foundation, Inc. 129:1966

Like Jackson Pollock and Willem De
Kooning, Mark Rothko was an important New York artist, whose highly abstract, gestural styles dominated American painting during the 1950s and 1960s.
This piece exemplifies Rothko's mature
work, which was characterized by large
dimensions and broad, cloud-like, often
brilliantly colored and beautifully modulated fields of paint.

In this canvas, the largest, central
cloud is bounded at the bottom by a
narrow area of acidic orange, and at the
top by the narrowest area of cool red.
The orange-red hue that borders these
areas, and over which they are painted,
serves to modulate the different values
of the colors. The artist's technique,
which involved staining the canvas with
pigment, makes the painting seem to
generate its own glowing light. Rothko
believed that the elimination of subject
matter and narrative references in his
paintings allowed the broad areas of color
to elicit a range of emotional responses
from the viewer.

Ellsworth Kelly, American, born 1923
Spectrum II, 1966–1967
Oil on canvas
80 x 273 in. (203.2 x 693.6 cm.)
Purchase: Funds given by the Shoenberg
Foundation, Inc. 4:1967

The American sculptor and painter
Ellsworth Kelly does not differentiate
between the two pursuits, finding each
serves a purpose in his exploration of
form. Kelly is a master of "hard edge"
painting, which seeks total unity in images with no foreground or background,
no "figures on a field."

During the 1950s and early 1960s,
Kelly explored the essential character of
seen phenomena, such as the shadows
and reflections created by a single shape
against a dark ground. His work from
this time concentrated on a large curved
form that pressed against the edges of the
canvas, seeming to extend beyond it. By
the later 1960s his shapes, whether rec-
tangles or flattened ovals, had become
more symmetrical, and he was working
increasingly with color.

In *Spectrum II,* Kelly has arranged
thirteen rectangular panels into a color or
"spectrum" chart. The color expands the
presence of the painting, which nearly
explodes into its surroundings, giving off
its own colored light and affecting all that
is near it. To reduce the figure-ground
relationship, Kelly is careful to show no
brushmarks. Along with the monumental scale of this work, its pristine surface
is characteristic of both Kelly's painting
and his sculpture from the 1950s to the
present.

David Smith, American, 1906–1965
Cubi XIV, 1963
Stainless steel
Height: 122½ in. (311.5 cm.)
Purchase: Friends Fund 32:1979

David Smith began work on his last sequence of sculptures, the *Cubi* series, in 1961, at his studio in New York. As in some of his earlier series, *Tanktotem, Voltri,* and *Agricola,* he numbered the works sequentially as he completed them. *Cubi XIV* was created just two years before the artist's death. The title of the series seems to refer to the early twentieth-century style, Cubism.

Unlike Smith's earlier series, the *Cubi*s are all geometrical elements of welded stainless steel. Welding allowed the artist to build his sculptures as he wished them to appear without resorting to casting or carving. Smith created, arranged, and assembled the units in upright relationships, subsequently scoring the surfaces with an electric sander. The friction of the grinding machine gave the metal an active, rich surface that recalls in *grisaille* both the shifting facets of Cubist paintings and the works of Smith's painter contemporaries, like Jackson Pollock.

The gestural surface of the sculpture contrasts with the austerity of the geometrical metal shapes. The blocky forms of the simple metal units of the *Cubi* series provided an important resource for the Minimalist sculptors of a younger generation, who abandoned the inflection of the artist's hand for the austerity and geometrical specificity of the shapes themselves. Smith's sculpture marks the intersection of the most important innovations in twentieth-century sculpture: the shifting faceted surface of Cubist paintings and the part-by-part methods of Constructivism.

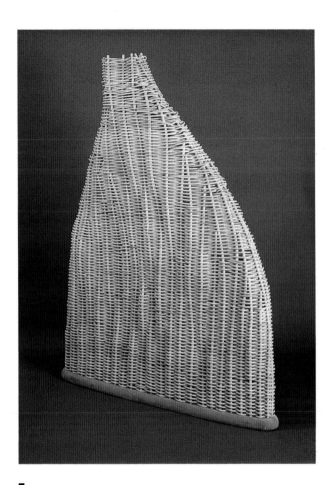

Martin Puryear, American, born 1941
The Charm of Subsistence, 1989
Rattan, gum wood
84¼ x 66 x 7½ in. (214 x 167.6 x 19 cm.)
Purchase: Funds given by the Shoenberg
Foundation, Inc. 105:1989

Martin Puryear describes himself as "a
builder, not a maker." In *The Charm of
Subsistence* he has worked with his own
hands to weave the heavy rattan, building the basket up from its base. Puryear's
style matured in the 1970s when Mini-
malism was prominent, and his work
acknowledges this movement through
the use of simple, restrained forms. However, the artist synthesizes a diversity of
sources and inspirations in his sculptures,
using materials and techniques that stem
from his life experiences.

In 1964–1966, Puryear spent two
years with the Peace Corps in Sierra Leone, West Africa, where he was exposed
to the indigenous craft traditions of a
pre-industrial society. In his subsequent
sculptures he has drawn on the forms he
saw used in the buildings and shelters
of this area, rather than the ceremonial
carvings which influenced previous
generations of artists. After his stay in
Sierra Leone, Puryear went to Stock-
holm, Sweden, to study printmaking and
sculpture. In Sweden he learned the arts
of wood joinery, boat building, and lami-
nating that later would play such a large
role in his work.

Chuck Close, American, born 1940
Keith, 1970
Acrylic on gessoed canvas
108¼ x 83¾ in. (275 x 212.5 cm.)
Purchase: Funds given by the Shoenberg
Foundation, Inc. 793:1983

Between 1968 and 1970, Chuck Close
painted seven large portraits of his
friends, all close-up views of their heads
done in *grisaille* (shades of gray), and all
based upon photographs the artist had
taken in his studio. The photographs
were gridded and, using an airbrush, the
artist then transferred the image to the
canvas.

Though *Keith* might seem to fit the
style known as photorealism, its direct-
ness of format, its large size, and the

impassive photographic image mediated
by the subjective hand of the artist bring
the work close to the mainstream of
advanced forms of contemporary art. It
has the characteristics of both a photograph and a traditional portrait painting,
and the ambitious scale of much of post-
War abstract American art.

While there is an unremitting stark-
ness to the painting and its bright white
background, there is also a lot of "information" in it. The subject's long hair,
turtleneck, informal shirt, and eyeglass
style are rooted in a particular time and
attitude. The highlights on the left side
of his head and the reflection of photographic lights in the lenses of his glasses
add a dynamic quality to a work that
may at first seem compelling but sphinx-
like.

Roy Lichtenstein, American, born 1923
Sailboats, 1985
Magna on canvas
120 x 96 in. (304.8 x 243.9 cm.)
Purchase: Funds given by the Shoenberg
Foundation, Inc. 10:1986

Roy Lichtenstein has based his compositions on the adoption and transformation
of established visual styles. From the
earliest codification in his cartoon images
of the 1960s, which appeared at once
redundant and completely inventive, he
has continued to pay homage to earlier
masters of the modern style.

Initially, *Sailboats* seems to be a huge
Fauve landscape painted eight decades
after the crucial "Fauve" year of 1905.
The viewer is perched precariously on a
hill above a beach, looking down at the
water and the sailboats to the right. The
painting, however, is far more complex
than it appears at first. It parodies not
only seminal innovations by painters
Matisse and Derain in the early years of
the twentieth century, but their own
dependence upon the flattened forms of
Japanese prints. The picture combines
the hard-edged "cartoon" brushstrokes of
the 1960s with the looser, more graphic
marks of Neo-Expressionism, which was
at its heyday in the early 1980s. The
painting also provides a commentary on
Lichtenstein as an observer and trans-
former of changing and permanent styles
of modern art.

Susan Rothenberg, American, born 1945
Mondrian Dancing, 1985
Oil on canvas
78¼ x 91 in. (200.6 x 233.3 cm.)
Purchase: Funds given by the Shoenberg
Foundation, Inc. 56:1985

The term "New Image Painting" was
coined during the 1970s to describe
works which, like Rothenberg's, include
figures and objects depicted in a gestural
manner by their essential forms and
shapes. Rothenberg's signature subject
became the horse, which seemed to
emerge in all her canvases amidst a
background of nuanced and abstracted
brushstrokes. By the 1980s she had incorporated the human figure into her work,
and with it references to personal memories and emotions.

Mondrian Dancing depicts the Dutch
modern painter and theoretician, one of
Rothenberg's most admired artists, dancing with a woman, perhaps in a Harlem
nightclub such as he liked to frequent.
Mondrian enjoyed jazz and dancing, and
in his last works, painted in New York,
his compositions referred to the synco-
pated rhythms of the Boogie-Woogie.
Rothenberg further evokes Mondrian's
presence with her select use of color: the
red, yellow, and blue that emerge from
the black and white ground are the primary colors we identify with the modern
master.

This is a romantic image, and perhaps
the artist imagined herself as the woman
dancing with her historical mentor. The
nearly life-size figures are swept to one
side of the composition by both the
movement of their dance and the broad
strokes of the artist's brush.

■
Gerhard Richter, German, born 1932
November, 1989
Oil on canvas
Diptych: 126 x 157½ in. (320 x 400 cm.)
Purchase: Funds given by Dr. and
Mrs. Alvin R. Frank and the Pulitzer
Publishing Foundation 30:1990

For many years, Gerhard Richter has
been working simultaneously in two
seemingly contradictory styles – abstraction and photorealism. In 1988, Richter
created a cycle of representational paintings entitled *18. Oktober 1977.* The grisaille paintings were derived from police
and newspaper photographs of the noto-
rious terrorists known as the Baader-
Meinhof Group whose mysterious deaths
on October 18, 1977 make up the subject
matter of these works. The final painting
in the series is a monumental image of
the group funeral given to these young
German intellectuals.

After completing this series of representational paintings, Richter made three
large abstract diptychs. They carry the
somber and elegiac mood of the *18. Oktober 1977* work. *November, December, Jan-
uary* follow the seasons from the fall into
the winter months. *November,* in particular, has the quality of a blurred, out-
of-focus photograph.

Richter's abstract paintings are made
in layers. First, a colorful base is freely
applied. Then Richter uses spatulas and
squeegees of various lengths to apply
subsequent layers. The results are large
vertical canvases which can be read as
layered patterns of paint under which
glow shimmering color or frozen winter
landscapes. The landscape, whether the
out-of-focus vision of a pine forest meeting a frozen lake (*November*) or the still,
refracted color of a frozen waterfall (*Jan-
uary*), connects these paintings to the
deathly stillness and silence of Richter's
Oktober paintings.

Anselm Kiefer, German, born 1948
Burning Rods, 1984–1987
Mixed media on canvas
130 x 219 x 11¾ in. (330.2 x 556.3 x 30 cm.)
Purchase: Gift of Mr. and Mrs. Joseph
Pulitzer, Jr., by exchange 108:1987

The meaning of this enormous landscape
is tightly intertwined with the theme of
Kiefer's painting *Osiris and Isis,* which
treats the ancient myth of the death and
dismemberment of the Egyptian god
Osiris, and his later rejuvenation.

The columnar rods in the central
panel, a symbol for the ravaging force of
nuclear power, are identified with a sequence of numerals ending in 14, a reference to the parts into which Osiris was
sundered. A gleaming bit of porcelain in
the right panel is an explicit connection
to the god, whose smashed form is
evoked in *Osiris and Isis* by porcelain
fragments.

The series of open boxes between the
rods and the cloud-like form in the sky
suggests the transition from the earth-
bound to the spiritual, a message reinforced by the rusty ice skate in the left
panel. The skate alludes to the passage
of the human spirit through time and
space, thus matching the role of the porcelain fragment, a tangible reminder of
the persistence of Osiris. In *Burning Rods,*
the artist, who may be Europe's leading
painter, has created a spiritual picture for
a secular age.

Index of Artists